T0193522

Reflections of
God's Law Books

JULIE RYAN

WESTBOW
PRESS®
A DIVISION OF THOMAS NELSON
& ZONDERVAN

WestBow Press books may be ordered through booksellers or by contacting:

WestBow Press
A Division of Thomas Nelson & Zondervan
1663 Liberty Drive
Bloomington, IN 47403
www.westbowpress.com
844-714-3454

ISBN: 978-1-6642-9578-0 (sc)
ISBN: 978-1-6642-9579-7 (hc)
ISBN: 978-1-6642-9577-3 (e)

Library of Congress Control Number: 2023905550

Print information available on the last page.

WestBow Press rev. date: 03/29/2023

I will study your commandments
and reflect on your ways.
—Psalm 119:15

Heavenly Father,
As I reflect on your Word,
help me to understand and apply
your truths to my life.
In Jesus's name I pray,

Amen

CONTENTS

Exodus

Leviticus

Numbers

Deuteronomy

✧ ✧ ✧

LAW BOOK 1

Genesis

GENESIS 1

Passage: "In the beginning, God created the heavens and the earth."

Reflection:

Creation—it's such a huge topic! But that's how God started this earth. How excited and thrilled the Trinity must have been bringing light and life to something that was dark and dead.

God's first words during creation were, "Let there be light." The lights were created to bring light to others, to govern, and to separate. And as children of God, that's also our role. While we live on this earth, we must let there be light in every aspect of our lives: our thoughts, words, and actions. For we know that God, our Father, is pure light. One day, when he replaces this earth with the new earth, there will be no need for the sun or moon. God himself will illuminate the earth with his glorious light as we live with him forever!

GENESIS 2

Passage: "Now the man and his wife were both naked, but they felt no shame."

Reflection:

This is a chapter of many firsts.

The first holy day of rest.

The first underground watering system, before God created rain.

The first human, a man formed by God from the dust.

The first warning from God; a violation would result in sin and death.

The first anesthesia.

The first operation performed by God himself.

The first woman created by God from man.

The first marriage between the man and the woman, his wife.

The man and woman were naked and felt no shame because they were sinless up to this point. It was like Heaven on earth at that time, pure and full of love, joy, and peace.

GENESIS 3

Passage: "'The serpent deceived me,' she replied. 'That's why I ate it.'"

Reflection:

This is when sin entered the world. Satan deceived Eve and caused her to doubt what God said. After she saw the forbidden tree and its fruit, she wanted it. She took it. She ate it. Then Eve gave the fruit to her husband, and he ate it. Their eyes were opened. They felt shame and hid from God when he called for them.

However, God killed an animal and shed its blood to provide a covering for their nakedness and shame from their sin. This is a picture of the sacrifice that Jesus would later make for the sins of the world.

Since this original sin, all people are infected with sin. But Jesus shed his blood for us. If we will accept him as our Savior, we are covered forever.

GENESIS 4

Passage: "The Lord accepted Abel and his gift, but he did not accept Cain and his gift."

Reflection:

Cain refused to do what God said was right, so the Lord did not accept him. People today think that they can do whatever they want and still be accepted by God. However, they are only saved by receiving the sacrifice of Jesus through faith. Thank God for the Bible where he clearly explains how we become his children.

GENESIS 5

Passage: "Methuselah lived 969 years, and then he died."

Reflection:

   With an average age of 846 years old, the lifespan of the people in Genesis 5 was about ten times as long as today's average lifespan. They didn't even start having children until they were sixty-five or older. They did not have lives of ease, comfort, and pleasure. Lamech named his son Noah, saying, "May he bring us relief from our work and the painful labor of farming this ground that the Lord cursed."

   Some people today would like to live 846 years or more on this earth. However, believers are blessed to have shorter lives so we can go to Heaven sooner and eternally live the truly good life with Jesus.

GENESIS 6

Passage: "The Lord observed the extent of human wickedness on the earth, and he saw that everything they thought or imagined was consistently and totally evil. So the Lord was sorry he had ever made them and put them on the earth. It broke his heart."

Reflection:

Do you ever think about God's heart being broken? According to the Bible, it happens when God sees wickedness in our thoughts. It doesn't even have to go as far as actions. It is what is in our hearts that breaks God's heart.

Sin starts in the mind, thoughts, and heart. Sin separates us from God. For the unsaved, sin separates them from a relationship with God. For the saved, sin separates them from fellowship with God. Ask God to point out anything that offends him, confess the sin in your heart, and ask the Holy Spirit to fill your mind with his thoughts.

GENESIS 7

Passage: "When everything was ready, the Lord said to Noah, 'Go into the boat with all your family, for among all the people of the earth, I can see that you alone are righteous.'"

Reflection:

Just as Noah and his family were allowed on the ark because they were the only righteous people on earth, only believers in Jesus Christ will be allowed to enter Heaven because only Jesus can make people righteous.

Just as the Lord closed the door to the ark, he will also close the door to Heaven, and those who do not enter will be destroyed.

GENESIS 8

Passage: "And the Lord was pleased with the aroma of the sacrifice and said to himself, 'I will never again curse the ground because of the human race, even though everything they think or imagine is bent toward evil from childhood. I will never again destroy all living things.'"

Reflection:

God tells us that everything the human race thinks or imagines is bent toward evil from childhood. Have you ever met someone who doesn't believe that he or she is a sinner? Everyone is a sinner from childhood. It's just a fact.

However, God loves sinners (not sin). He sent his Son, Jesus, to offer the perfect, eternal sacrifice of his life for our sins. Jesus's blood pays for our sins, past, present, and future. No more sacrifices are needed.

The only thing we need to do is agree with God that we are sinners, believe in Jesus, and accept him as our Savior. We don't have to sacrifice anything; Jesus did that for us with his body.

GENESIS 9

Passage: "Then God said to Noah, 'Yes, this rainbow is the sign of the covenant I am confirming with all the creatures on earth.'"

Reflection:

Because God made human beings in his own image, he requires the blood of anyone who takes another person's life. Even if a wild animal kills a person, it must die. And if anyone takes a human life, that person's life will also be taken by human hands. This applies to murder inside or outside the womb.

After God wiped out every living thing on earth with a flood, he promised that never again would flood waters destroy all life. God placed his rainbow in the clouds as a sign of the eternal covenant between him and every living creature on earth. This is the true meaning of the rainbow.

GENESIS 10

Passage: "All the nations of the earth descended from these clans after the great flood."

Reflection:

Since the flood destroyed all people except for Noah and his three sons and their wives, we can all trace our ancestry back to one of Noah's sons. All the nations of the earth descended from Shem, Ham, and Japheth. Abram (Abraham) is a descendant of Shem.

GENESIS 11

Passage: "At one time all the people of the world spoke the same language and used the same words."

Reflection:

People have a tendency not to want change. They like to stay around familiar people and do the things they are used to doing. This is similar to when all people spoke the same language and settled together near Babylonia. The people were comfortable there in Babel, so God had to confuse them by making them speak different languages to get them to scatter all over the world.

Sometimes change can be confusing and painful. However, if it gets us to move in a different direction that puts us in line with God's will, the result is good.

GENESIS 12

Passage: "Abram said to his wife, Sarai, 'Look, you are a very beautiful woman. When the Egyptians see you, they will say, "This is his wife. Let's kill him; then we can have her!" So please tell them you are my sister. Then they will spare my life and treat me well because of their interest in you.'"

Reflection:

When Abram (later to be called Abraham) was called by God, the Lord told him to leave his country and his relatives and go to the place that God would show him. Abram did as the Lord had instructed. He packed up everything and left Haran. As he traveled and set up camps, Abram built altars that he dedicated to the Lord, and he worshipped God. Although he was not perfect, Abram's life was characterized by faith in God, obedience to God, and worship of God. As Christians, this should be what our lives look like too.

However, fear got the best of Abram when he and Sarai, his wife, entered Egypt. God quickly intervened and sent plagues upon Pharaoh and his household, correcting the mistake that Abram had made in allowing Pharaoh to take Sarai as his wife.

When we fail to trust God, we can make a mess of things, but God will move Heaven and earth to rescue us and keep his plan moving forward.

GENESIS 13

Passage: "Take your choice of any section of any section of the land you want, and we will separate."

Reflection:

As believers, we have faith that God will work all things out for our good. We know that God controls all things. When Abram and his nephew, Lot, decided to separate because the land couldn't support both of their herds of cattle, sheep, and goats, Abram told Lot to choose whatever land he wanted. Abram trusted that God would make sure he went to the land chosen for him by God. There was no arguing or fighting, just a peaceful separation.

After Lot left to settle in the land near Sodom, God rewarded Abram's belief and told him he was giving all the land as far as he could see to Abram and his countless descendants. God continued to bless Abram; Abram built another altar in Hebron and continued to worship God. What a loving relationship!

GENESIS 14

Passage: "Blessed be Abram by God Most High, Creator of heaven and earth. And blessed be God Most High, who has defeated your enemies for you."

Reflection:

When Lot, Abram's nephew, was captured by an army of invaders in Sodom, Abram acted quickly and courageously. Abram pursued the army of Kedorlaomer with 318 men who were born into his household. They attacked during the night, the army fled, and Abram brought back Lot and the other captives as well as their possessions.

Melchizadek, the king of Salem and a priest, blessed Abram, saying, "Blessed be Abram by God Most High." All the glory of Abram's victory belonged to God, just as it does when God gives us victory in our day-to-day lives. When we are blessed by God, God deserves our blessing.

GENESIS 15

Passage: "And Abram believed the Lord, and the Lord counted him as righteous because of his faith."

Reflection:

Because of Abram's faith in God, God promised Abram:

- I will protect you;
- Your reward will be great;
- You will have a son;
- Your descendants will be as numerous as the stars in the sky, but they will be slaves in a foreign land for 400 years;
- I will punish the nation that enslaved them, and in the end they will come away with great wealth;
- You will die in peace at a ripe old age; and
- After four generations, your descendants will return to their God-given land.

GENESIS 16

Passage: "This son of yours will be a wild man, as untamed as a wild donkey! He will raise his fist against everyone, and everyone will be against him. Yes, he will live in open hostility against his relatives."

Reflection:

Being impatient and failing to wait for God to unfold his plans leads to trouble. Sarai had tried for at least ten years to conceive a child with Abram, when she had the not-so-bright idea of Abram having a child through her servant, Hagar.

Abram did as Sarai suggested, which resulted in bad feelings between Sarai, Hagar, and Abram. Nevertheless, the Lord, who sees and hears everything, loved Hagar and went to her in her distress. He revealed that her son (who is associated with Arabs today) would be a wild man who would raise his fist against everyone.

The Lord told Hagar to name her son Ishmael, and so Abram named him as God had said. Even today, the conflict continues with Abram's son, Ishmael.

GENESIS 17

Passage: "But God replied, 'No—Sarah, your wife, will give birth to a son for you. You will name him Isaac, and I will confirm my covenant with him and his descendants as an everlasting covenant.'"

Reflection:

When Abram was ninety-nine years old and his son Ishmael was thirteen, God changed Abram's name to Abraham and Sarai's name to Sarah. God said that Abraham and Sarah would give birth to a son in about a year. Abraham was to name him Isaac. God would confirm his everlasting covenant of special blessing with Isaac and his descendants.

The promises of God included countless descendants. Abraham would be the father of many nations, and kings would be among them. He would be extremely fruitful. God would always be the God of him and his descendants, and God would give the entire land of Canaan to them forever.

The responsibility of Abraham and his descendants was to obey God and be circumcised. Circumcision did not make Abraham accepted by God. It was a sign that Abraham already had faith, and that God had already accepted him and declared him to be righteous even before he was circumcised.

When we come to Christ, we are circumcised, but not by a physical procedure. Christ performed a spiritual circumcision: the cutting away of our sinful natures. Abraham is the spiritual father of those who have faith but have not been circumcised. They are counted as righteous because of their faith.

GENESIS 18

Passage: "The Lord appeared again to Abraham near the oak grove belonging to Mamre."

Reflection:

The Lord Jesus came down from Heaven and ate with Abraham. He announced that Sarah would have a son and when she laughed to herself, he said, "Is anything too hard for the Lord? I will return about this time next year, and Sarah will have a son." The Lord also said that he came to see if the sin in Sodom and Gomorrah was as bad as the great outcry he had heard. How awesome!

As early as Genesis, Jesus was here with his people, Abraham and Sarah. What a loving and caring God! Even though we can't see him physically, like Abraham did, Jesus is here with his people, living in us through the Holy Spirit. We can have constant fellowship with him. We walk in the Lord's presence as we live here on earth. We are never alone.

GENESIS 19

Passage: "But God had listened to Abraham's request and kept Lot safe, removing him from the disaster that engulfed the cities on the plain."

Reflection:

Before God answered the outcry against the cities of Sodom and Gomorrah with destruction, God gave a warning through two angels to Lot about the coming destruction and how to escape to safety. Lot believed the angels, accepted the offer, and left Sodom without looking back. God was merciful to Lot and saved his life just as his uncle Abraham had requested.

This event mirrors salvation. God has warned us in the Bible about the future destruction to come on earth and the eternal destruction in Hell. God has told us how to escape to eternal life in Heaven through faith in Jesus. It is up to us to believe and accept God's offer of salvation.

Once we do accept Jesus as our Savior and Lord, we are not to look back longingly at our past lives but move forward with a commitment to follow Jesus. Our prayers for the unsaved do matter, as God shows mercy and offers salvation to them.

GENESIS 20

Passage: "But that night God came to Abimelech in a dream and told him, 'You are a dead man for that woman you have taken is already married!'"

Reflection:

Abraham was still fearful of being killed. He had not yet learned to fully trust God for protection. That is why he deceived Abimelech, letting him believe that Sarah was only his sister and not his wife, just as he had done in the past.

Can you imagine being Abimelech and hearing God say, "You are a dead man, for that woman you have taken is already married"? God even caused Abimelech's other wife and his female servants to be infertile because of what happened with Sarah. However, since Abimelech was innocent in the matter and made things right with God by returning Sarah to Abraham without touching her, God spared Abimelech's life and healed the women so they could have children.

Don't be afraid. Trust God to take care of you. Don't deceive others. Be faithful to your spouse.

GENESIS 21

Passage: "The Lord kept his word and did for Sarah exactly what he had promised. She became pregnant, and she gave birth to a son for Abraham in his old age. This happened at just the time God had said it would."

Reflection:

Here is another great example of God's faithfulness to his word. Whatever God says, we can believe it will be fulfilled completely. Read the book of Revelation. It will be fulfilled one hundred percent. Read any promise of God in the Bible; it will be totally fulfilled. The Bible and its Author can be trusted entirely.

GENESIS 22

Passage: "Then Abraham looked up and saw a ram caught by its horns in a thicket. So he took the ram and sacrificed it as a burnt offering in place of his son."

Reflection:

Here is an example of perfect obedience. When God told Abraham to sacrifice his only son Isaac as a burnt offering, he got up early the next morning and proceeded to go do what God had commanded. There is no evidence between verses 2 and 3 that Abraham questioned, complained, or argued with God. He simply obeyed God.

This is the kind of obedience that pleases God. He said to Abraham, "Because you have obeyed me and have not withheld even your son, your only son, I swear by my own name that I will certainly bless you." This is the kind of obedience that God wants from us. It is also the same kind of obedience that Jesus had to his Father.

This is an example of how God would later sacrifice his Son, his only Son, Jesus, whom he loved so much. Yahweh-Yireh (which means "the Lord will provide") provided Jesus, pictured as the ram, as a substitute sacrifice for us so we would not need to die for our sins.

GENESIS 23

Passage: "Choose the finest of our tombs and bury her there."

Reflection:

When Sarah died at the age of 127 at Hebron in the land of Canaan, Abraham was in need of a place to bury her. Even though he was a stranger and a foreigner there, God caused Abraham to be honored among the Hittite elders. God not only provided the cave that Abraham wanted as a family burial place, but also the field that the cave was in and all the surrounding trees.

Our loving and generous God not only meets the needs of his beloved children, but he also provides the finest of blessings for them.

GENESIS 24

Passage: "Before he had finished praying, he saw a young woman named Rebekah coming out with her water jug on her shoulder."

Reflection:

God knows what we need before we do and is already working on it. Before Abraham's servant had finished praying, God answered his prayer and sent Rebekah to the well. Because of God's unfailing love and faithfulness, he leads us every day, as he led Abraham's servant straight to Rebekah and Abraham's relatives. Rebekah's brother and father immediately obeyed God and agreed to let her become Isaac's wife. Rebekah obeyed and did not hesitate to go to Canaan.

Abraham had faith that the Lord would send his angel with his servant and would make his mission successful, and he did. God does the same thing for us, his faithful children. He will make our missions successful too.

GENESIS 25

Passage: "Abraham lived for 175 years, and he died at a ripe old age, having lived a long and satisfying life. He breathed his last and joined his ancestors in death."

Reflection:

Isn't this the kind of ending we would like? Abraham was blessed by God!

Esau, Isaac's firstborn son, on the other hand was not so blessed. He sold his rights as the firstborn to his brother Jacob for some stew and bread in a moment of weakness. Learn from Esau and be careful of doing or saying things that you will later regret in times of weakness and vulnerability, like when you are hungry or exhausted.

GENESIS 26

Passage: "When Isaac planted his crops that year, he harvested a hundred times more grain than he planted, for the Lord blessed him."

Reflection:

A severe famine caused Isaac to move to Gerar, where the Lord appeared to him and said, "I will be with you and bless you." The Lord appeared to Isaac again in Beersheba on the night of his arrival and said, "Do not be afraid, for I am with you and will bless you." Perhaps Isaac needed reassurance that he was doing the right thing and living in the right place, according to God's will. Both times God confirmed his presence and his blessing to Isaac.

As God's children, we also can be assured of his presence with us as he guides us each day. No matter where we live, when we are living in God's will, we are living in a place of blessing.

GENESIS 27

Passage: "Isaac began to tremble uncontrollably and said, 'Then who just served me wild game? I have already eaten it, and I blessed him just before you came. And yes, that blessing must stand!'"

Reflection:

Earlier, God told Rebekah, while the twins were still in her womb, that her older son would serve her younger son. The older son, Esau, gave away his firstborn rights for some food. Isaac gave his firstborn blessing to Jacob instead of Esau, saying "May many nations become your servants, and may they bow down to you. May you be the master over your brothers and may your mother's sons bow down to you. All who curse you will be cursed, and all who bless you will be blessed."

Things always happen just as God says. He plans the future and knows exactly how it will unfold. So believe him, believe Jesus, the living Word, and believe the Bible, the written Word.

GENESIS 28

Passage: "Surely the Lord is in this place, and I wasn't even aware of it!"

Reflection:

As with his father Isaac, God came to Jacob in a dream. God showed him a stairway to Heaven with angels going up and down and the Lord standing at the top of the stairway. The Lord confirmed with Jacob his blessing of land, many descendants, his protection, and presence. The next morning, Jacob made a memorial pillar using the stone that he had rested his head against. In addition, Jacob vowed that the Lord would be his God and he promised to give God back a tenth of everything that he was given.

As Christians, we should also follow Jacob's example and give God back a tenth of what he gives us. As we recognize that everything comes from God and develop a spirit of thankfulness and generosity, we will surely be blessed. You can't out-give God.

GENESIS 29

Passage: "When the Lord saw that Leah was unloved, he enabled her to have children."

Reflection:

God cares deeply about his children and here is another example of his love. Because Jacob loved Rachel, God blessed Leah with many sons to surround her with love. Like Leah, God sees us too. He knows how those close to us feel about us and treat us, and whether we are truly loved or if we are just being used.

God wants us to have genuine, loving relationships with him first, with our brothers and sisters in Christ, and with others in our lives. God will meet our need for love in ways that are perfect for us.

GENESIS 30

Passage: "You had little indeed before I came, but your wealth has increased enormously. The Lord has blessed you through everything I've done."

Reflection:

As a result of the competition, jealousy, and impatience between Leah and Rachel, God blessed Jacob with many sons. Despite Laban's dishonest manipulation, God also blessed Jacob with wealth, large flocks of sheep and goats, servants, camels, and donkeys.

God can turn the negative motives of others into blessings for his chosen ones.

GENESIS 31

Passage: "But the God of my father has been with me."

Reflection:

God's love and faithfulness to Jacob is demonstrated repeatedly. Jacob recognized it. When referring to his father-in-law Laban, he said, "But God has not allowed him to do me any harm…God has taken your father's animals and given them to me…But God has seen your abuse and my hard work. Also, God appeared to Laban in a dream as he was in hot pursuit of Jacob and said, "I'm warning you—leave Jacob alone!"

As faithful believers, Almighty God is our provider and protector too. We have no reason to fear because God is watching over us and he will do whatever it takes to bless us and keep us safe.

GENESIS 32

Passage: "As Jacob started on his way again, angels of God came to meet him."

Reflection:

Wow! What an awesome sight that must have been. God was pleased with Jacob after his meeting and covenant not to harm Laban. Jacob was humble and thankful to God for his unfailing love and faithfulness. He said, "When I left home and crossed the Jordan river, I owned nothing except a walking stick. Now my household fills two large camps!" Later, the Lord changed Jacob's name to Israel and blessed him.

This is what can happen in our lives when we follow the Lord: blessing upon blessing. God wants to bless his children and does amazing things for us still today. The God of Abraham, Isaac, and Jacob is my God, and he is the same yesterday, today, and forever!

Reading: **GENESIS 33**

Passage: "Then Esau ran to meet him and embraced him, threw his arms around his neck, and kissed him. And they both wept."

Reflection:

The reconciliation of Jacob and Esau is similar to the father's forgiveness in the story of the prodigal son in Luke 15, except the Old Testament story is between brothers. This is how believers should forgive others, especially our brothers and sisters in Christ.

GENESIS 34

Passage: "So all the men in the town council agreed with Hamor and Shechem, and every male in the town was circumcised. But three days later, when their wounds were still sore, two of Jacob's sons, Simeon and Levi, who were Dinah's full brothers, took their swords and entered the town without opposition."

Reflection:

Dinah, the daughter of Jacob and Leah, was seized and raped by Prince Shechem. No matter who it is, this is "something that should never be done." Because Shechem had defiled their sister, Dinah's brothers took justice into their own hands. They deceived Shechem and his father, slaughtered every male with their swords, plundered the town, and took their children and wives as captives.

GENESIS 35

Passage: "Then God said, 'I am El-Shaddai — "God Almighty." Be fruitful and multiply. You will become a great nation, even many nations. Kings will be among your descendants! And I will give you the land I once gave to Abraham and Isaac. Yes, I will give it to you and your descendants after you.'"

Reflection:

Jacob was going back to Bethel (which means "house of God") to settle. He planned to "build an altar to the God who answered my prayers when I was in distress. He has been with me wherever I have gone." El-Shaddai, God Almighty, appeared to Jacob again at Bethel, spoke to him, and blessed him.

An altar is a sacred place to worship, honor, and offer gifts to God. As Christians, we should have our own altars, special places where we meet with God, read his Word, worship him, and offer gifts of prayer and thanksgiving. God will meet us there every day and bless us.

GENESIS 36

Passage: "These are the leaders of the clans of Edom, listed according to their settlements in the land they occupied. They all descended from Esau, the ancestor of the Edomites."

Reflection:

Esau, also known as Edom, and his brother Jacob, also known as Israel, have been in conflict since the book of Genesis, throughout the Bible, and today. Edom refused to allow Israel to pass through in Numbers. God speaks of the destruction of Edom in Jeremiah and Obadiah. David speaks of victory over Edom in Psalms.

The Ishmael and Esau descendants of Abraham are still in conflict with the Isaac and Jacob descendants of Abraham. Regardless of which side of the family of Abraham we are from, all people are created by God, in his image, and he loves them. God wants everyone to accept his son Jesus and his sacrifice on the cross for their sins. Only then can we call ourselves true children of God and look forward to living together with our Father in Heaven forever.

GENESIS 37

Passage: "'Listen to this dream,' he said. 'We were out in the field, tying up bundles of grain. Suddenly my bundle stood up, and your bundles all gathered around and bowed low before mine!'"

Reflection:

In the process of fulfilling the dreams that God gave Joseph about others bowing low to him, God used the hate of his brothers as a tool to get Joseph to Egypt. God took Joseph from tending his father's flocks of sheep in Canaan to Potiphar, an officer of Pharaoh, the king of Egypt.

God never left Joseph. He protected him every step of the way.

GENESIS 38

Passage: "But as they were taking her out to kill her, she sent this message to her father-in-law: 'The man who owns these things made me pregnant. Look closely. Whose seal and cord and walking stick are these?'"

Reflection:

Judah's sons, Er and Onan, were wicked in the Lord's eyes, so the Lord took their lives. Even though birth and death seem to occur naturally, it is God who gives life and takes it away.

Judah propositioned Tamar, his daughter-in-law, to have sex with him, not realizing that she was disguised as a prostitute. However, three months later, when someone told Judah that Tamar was pregnant because she had acted like a prostitute, he said, "Bring her out and let her be burned!" When the truth came out that Judah was the father of her twins, he said, "She is more righteous than I am." In that case, Judah should have been burned!

Jesus, the descendant of Judah and Tamar, sacrificed his life so that no one has to burn. He did not teach us to condemn or judge others, but instead to forgive them, just as he forgives and makes righteous anyone who accepts him as their Savior and Lord.

GENESIS 39

Passage: "The Lord was with him and caused everything he did to succeed."

Reflection:

Why was Joseph successful in everything he did? Because the Lord was with him and caused him to succeed. This point is emphasized four times in this chapter.

When you are a faithful child of God, he will show you his faithful love wherever he places you. As God blessed Potiphar's household for Joseph's sake, he will bless others (your workplace, your family) for your sake. Living and working with faithful Christians is a good strategy for success because others benefit from our relationships with God.

GENESIS 40

Passage: "And please remember me and do me a favor when things go well for you. Mention me to Pharaoh, so he might let me out of this place."

Reflection:

Joseph was in prison and did nothing to deserve it. While he was there, he was put in charge of all the other prisoners and everything that happened in the prison because God caused the warden to favor him. Even in prison, Joseph continued to grow, bud, and blossom. Because God had a plan and purpose for Joseph, it was his will to put him there to serve at that time in his life.

One way Joseph served was by interpreting dreams for Pharaoh's cup bearer and baker, who were both in prison too. Joseph asked the cup bearer to remember him when he returned to work for Pharaoh but "he never gave him another thought." However, God was still in control.

No matter where God puts you to serve, even in prison, you are to work willingly and with enthusiasm, as though you are working for the Lord rather than for people.

GENESIS 41

Passage: "And people from all around came to Egypt to buy grain from Joseph because the famine was severe throughout the world."

Reflection:

Two years after Joseph asked the cup bearer to remember him, the cup bearer was reminded of his failure when Pharaoh had two dreams that no one could interpret. With God's power, Joseph was able to accurately tell Pharaoh what his dreams meant: seven years of prosperity followed by seven years of famine.

Joseph advised Pharaoh just what he should do to ensure there would be enough food during the seven years of famine, and his suggestions were well received. Recognizing that Joseph was filled with the spirit of God and that no one else was as intelligent or wise, Pharaoh said, "I hereby put you in charge of the entire land of Egypt." Joseph was thirty years old. Pharaoh also gave Joseph a wife, the daughter of a priest, and they had two sons, Manasseh and Ephraim.

God orchestrated all these events, from the cup bearer being imprisoned where Joseph was to Joseph being made second in rank just below Pharaoh. Before the beginning of time, God wrote our life stories and the story of the world. Page by page, history unfolds just as God has planned. Nothing happens by chance. As his children, we can trust God to bring us through to the happily-ever-after ending written in the book of Revelation!

GENESIS 42

Passage: "When they arrived, they bowed before him with their faces to the ground."

Reflection:

Joseph's brothers traveled from Canaan to Egypt to buy grain. Joseph recognized his brothers instantly and remembered the dreams he had about them bowing to him many years before. The dreams that Joseph shared with his brothers when he was seventeen came true about thirteen years later.

God was with Joseph the entire time, grooming him for this position at this time. Joseph did not reveal his identity at once, but he treated his brothers with kindness. He ordered his servants to give them grain and supplies for their journey home, and secretly returned their money to each of them. Joseph kept Simeon in jail while he waited for his little brother Benjamin to come to Egypt. His older brothers promised they would get him, still not knowing that they were speaking to Joseph.

GENESIS 43

Passage: "Relax. Don't be afraid."

Reflection:

The brothers were terrified when they saw that they were being taken into Joseph's house. "It's because of the money someone put in our sacks last time we were here," they said. "He plans to pretend that we stole it. Then he will seize us, making us slaves, and taking our donkeys."

Here we see Joseph's brothers imagining the worst-case scenario as to why they were being taken into Joseph's palace. How often do we think the same way? Compare what they thought would happen to what actually happened –

> Joseph told each of his brothers where to sit, to their amazement, he seated them according to age, from the oldest to the youngest. And Joseph filled their plates with food from his own table, giving Benjamin five times as much as he gave the others. So they feasted and drank freely with him.

We should listen to the words that the household manager told Joseph's brothers instead of imagining the worst. God is good.

GENESIS 44

Passage: "The cup was found in Benjamin's sack! When the brothers saw this, they tore their clothing in despair."

Reflection:

It is difficult to read about Joseph putting his silver cup in Benjamin's sack and then telling the palace manager to accuse them of stealing it. It seems cruel to cause so much mental anguish to his brothers until you remember what they did to Joseph.

Joseph was sold by his brothers to Ishmaelite traders and taken away from his father for more than thirteen years. This caused both Joseph and Jacob a lot of mental anguish. Judah was correct when he said, "God is punishing us for our sins."

GENESIS 45

Passage: "Joseph could stand it no longer. 'I am Joseph!' But his brothers were speechless! They were stunned to realize that Joseph was standing there in front of them."

Reflection:

Wow! What a great surprise and reunion between Joseph and his brothers. *God* sent Joseph to Egypt, which Joseph emphasized three times to his brothers. God had planned all along to make Joseph master over the land of Egypt to keep Jacob's family and many other people alive during the seven years of famine. God made Pharaoh respond with kindness and generosity to Joseph's brothers, saying, "the best of all the land of Egypt is yours."

Can you imagine the excitement during the trip back to Canaan to tell Jacob that his son Joseph was alive? Jacob was stunned when he heard the news, just like Joseph's brothers were. However, they readily believed it after seeing all the wagons that Joseph sent to carry his many relatives back to Egypt. Jacob said, "It must be true! My son Joseph is alive! I must go and see him before I die."

Like David said later in Psalm 30, "You have turned my mourning into joyful dancing. You have taken away my clothes of mourning and clothed me with joy."

GENESIS 46

Passage: "The total number of Jacob's direct descendants who went with him to Egypt, not counting his sons' wives, was sixty-six. In addition, Joseph had two sons who were born in Egypt. So altogether, there were seventy members of Jacob's family in the land of Egypt."

Reflection:

As Jacob was moving to Egypt, God spoke to him in a vision one night when he was in Beersheba. He said, "I am God, the God of your father. Do not be afraid to go down to Egypt, for there I will make your family into a great nation. I will go with you down to Egypt, and I will bring you back again. You will die in Egypt, but Joseph will be with you to close your eyes."

How loving God was to ease Jacob's mind about his future in Egypt. God still speaks to his children today, reassuring us of his presence, power, and protection. Whatever fears we may have, God provides comfort and peace of mind if we pause long enough to focus on him and listen to him.

GENESIS 47

Passage: "'You have saved our lives,' they exclaimed. 'May it please you, my lord, to let us be Pharaoh's servants.'"

Reflection:

In exchange for food from Joseph during the famine, the people of the lands of Egypt and Canaan gave him their money, livestock, land, and themselves. They surrendered everything for life.

Jesus gave us his very own life on the cross so that we can have eternal life. Doesn't it make sense that we should surrender all to him?

GENESIS 48

Passage: "So Jacob blessed the boys that day with this blessing: 'The people of Israel will use your names when they give a blessing. They will say, "May God make you as prosperous as Ephraim and Manasseh."' In this way, Jacob put Ephraim ahead of Manasseh."

Reflection:

When Jacob's health was failing, Joseph went to him and took his two sons, Ephraim and Manasseh. Jacob said, "Now I am claiming as my own sons these two boys of yours…they will be my sons, just as Reuben and Simeon are." That is why Israel has a tribe of Ephraim and Manasseh. Jacob claimed his grandsons as sons.

Even though Jacob was almost blind, God caused him to cross his arms, put his right hand on the younger son, Ephraim, and bless him before the older son. Even if we are nearly blind or disabled, God will accomplish his will. What we think is the right way to do something may be totally opposite of how God wants it to be done.

GENESIS 49

Passage: "May the God of your father help you; may the Almighty bless you with the blessings of the heavens above, and blessings of the watery depths below, and blessings of the breasts and womb. May my fatherly blessings on you surpass the blessings of my ancestors, reaching to the heights of the eternal hills. May these blessings rest on the head of Joseph, who is a prince among his brothers."

Reflection:

Before Jacob died, he said to his sons, "Gather around me, and I will tell you what will happen to each of you in the days to come." To some of his sons, Jacob gave blessings and told them of a future to look forward to. However, to Reuben he said, "You will be first no longer. For you went to bed with my wife. You defiled my marriage couch." This incident is barely mentioned in Genesis 35:22, but it comes out here and affects Reuben's entire future.

Jacob then cursed the anger, wrath, and cruelty of Simeon and Levi. Judah and Joseph received the best blessings. Zebulun, Issachar, Dan, Gad, Asher, Naphtali, and Benjamin all received appropriate blessings—neither great nor bad.

If God told you what would happen in your future days, what group would you be in? Reuben, Simeon, and Levi? Judah and Joseph? Zebulun, Issachar, Dan, Gad, Asher, Naphtali, and Benjamin?

GENESIS 50

Passage: "Don't be afraid of me. Am I God that I can punish you? You intended to harm me, but God intended it all for good. He brought me to this position so I could save the lives of many people. No, don't be afraid. I will continue to take care of you and your children."

Reflection:

Joseph was such a godly man. After all he had been through, because of his brothers' cruelty, he spoke kindly and reassured them. What an example of forgiveness. It's like Jesus forgiving the people who crucified him as he hung on the cross. They intended not only to harm but to kill Jesus. However, God intended it for good, to save the lives of many people, including you and me, through the blood of his only Son.

✧ ✧ ✧

LAW BOOK 2

Exodus

EXODUS 1

Passage: "We must make a plan to keep them from growing even more. If we don't, and if war breaks out, they will join our enemies and fight against us."

Reflection:

After Joseph and his brothers died in Egypt and a new Pharaoh came to power, things turned bad for the Israelites. Since the new Pharaoh didn't know anything about Joseph or what he had done, he was afraid of the size and strength of the Israelites. Therefore, Pharaoh made them slaves, oppressing them with crushing labor and brutal slave drivers. Instead of decreasing in size, the Israelites multiplied and spread. Pharaoh then ordered that every newborn Hebrew boy be thrown into the Nile River.

Even today, from generation to generation, things change, and not always for the better. As the lessons of the Bible are not passed down or are forgotten, Satan causes people to fear and feel threatened by Christians, and even view a biblical worldview as radical. Just as Joseph was not remembered in Egypt for what he had done to save the lives of many people, neither is Jesus Christ remembered for what he did to save the lives of all people. This leads to society wanting to remove, censor, restrict, cancel, and eliminate Christianity altogether.

EXODUS 2

Passage: "God heard their groaning, and he remembered his covenant promise to Abraham, Isaac, and Jacob. He looked down on the people of Israel and knew it was time to act."

Reflection:

Moses's parents, both from the tribe of Levi, knew that he was a special baby and kept him hidden for three months. God had great plans for Moses, and he was not going to let anything happen to him. God arranged for him to be adopted by Pharaoh's daughter as her own son. God loves adoption. He even adopts us into his own family when we believe in and accept his Son Jesus as our Savior and Lord.

Moses knew he was a Hebrew. When he saw an Egyptian beating a Hebrew slave, he felt sorry for the Hebrew and killed the Egyptian. Then Moses fled to Midian where he married Zipporah, the daughter of the priest of Midian. They had a son named Gershom.

The king of Egypt died, and the Israelites cried out to God for help because of their burden of slavery. God hears us, God sees us, and God will act, when it's time.

EXODUS 3

Passage: "Then the Lord told him, 'I have certainly seen the oppression of my people in Egypt. I have heard their cries of distress.'"

Reflection:

God really knows how to get our attention. If he needs to, he will appear in the middle of a bush that looks like it's burning, as he did with Moses. Whatever it takes, God will get our attention when he has something to say. Again the Lord said that he saw, heard, and was aware of the suffering of the Israelites in Egypt. He came down to rescue them and lead them out to their own land. God came down to do this because he is so loving, faithful, and good!

The Lord told Moses that he "must lead my people Israel out of Egypt." See how good God is to his people. What an honor to be considered one of them! There's nothing too big that God won't do for us. Then God reassured Moses that he would be with him, just as he is with us who belong to Jesus today.

Since God knew what the future would bring, because he planned it, he was able to tell Moses that the Israelites would accept his message. However, the king of Egypt would not let them go unless a mighty hand forced him. Sometimes people today are stubborn, and

God needs to strike them with his mighty hand to wake them up so that they will repent and come to him for restoration or salvation. God explained that he would strike the Egyptians with many miracles and finally the king would let the Israelites go. And after stripping the Egyptians of their silver, gold, and fine clothing, the Israelites would leave Egypt. God will supply all our needs too, just as he did for his people, the Israelites.

EXODUS 4

Passage: "But Moses protested again, 'What if they won't believe me or listen to me? What if they say, "The Lord never appeared to you?"'"

Reflection:

How often do we respond to a directive from God with "what if?" Rather than trusting God, we imagine future scenarios without God's help and worry about what could happen. Don't let the fear of "what if" prevent you from obeying God and moving forward. The Lord told Moses, "Now go! I will be with you as you speak, and I will instruct you in what to say...and do." Trust God to do the same for you today. Now go!

EXODUS 5

Passage: "And who is the Lord? Why should I listen to him and let Israel go? I don't know the Lord, and I will not let Israel go."

Reflection:

Sometimes those who do not know the Lord Jesus Christ treat his people with contempt, just like Pharaoh did to the Israelites. You can hear the unbelieving world saying the same thing today: "Who is the Lord? Why should I listen to him? I don't know the Lord, and I will not" do what is asked. That is why Christians need to tell people about Jesus so they can know the Lord.

The Bible says that believers in Jesus are a dreadful smell of death and doom to those who are perishing. To those who are being saved, we are a life-giving perfume. The Israelite foremen were correct when they said to Moses and Aaron that they "stink before Pharaoh and his officials."

But God wasn't finished yet, and Pharaoh was getting ready to find out who the Lord was!

EXODUS 6

Passage: "I am Yahweh—the Lord, I appeared to Abraham, Isaac, and to Jacob as El-Shaddai—God Almighty—but I did not reveal my name, Yahweh, to them."

Reflection:

"I will free you." God promised to free the Israelites from their oppression. Jesus will free us from our oppression of sin and death.

"I will rescue you." God promised to rescue the Israelites from their slavery in Egypt. Jesus will rescue us from the bondage of sin.

"I will redeem you." God promised to redeem the Israelites with a powerful arm and great acts. Jesus redeemed us when he died on the cross, but we must accept his payment for our sin and ask him to be our Savior.

"I will claim you." God claimed the Israelites as his own people. Jesus claims us as the bride of Christ (and children of God) when we receive his gift of salvation.

"I will be your God." God promised the Israelites to always be their God. Jesus, who is God the Son, will always be with us and be our God.

"I will bring you." God promised to bring the Israelites into the land promised to Abraham, Isaac, and Jacob. Jesus promises to bring us to the promised land of Heaven.

"I will give it to you." God promised the Israelites the land of Canaan as their own possession. Jesus promises an inheritance of Heaven and everything in it for the children of God.

EXODUS 7

Passage: "But I will make Pharaoh's heart stubborn so I can multiply my miraculous signs and wonders in the land of Egypt."

Reflection:

God is always in control, and he has a reason for everything. Why did he make Pharaoh's heart stubborn? It was so he could do more miraculous signs in Egypt. Why? He did it for the good of the Egyptian people. God wanted them to know that he was the Lord: "When I raise my powerful hand and bring out the Israelites, the Egyptians will know that I am the Lord."

You are never too old to start serving the Lord. Moses was eighty years old when he went to Pharaoh with his brother Aaron. Two-thirds of Moses's life was over, but God gave him forty more years of good health so he could continue to serve him.

EXODUS 8

Passage: "But this time I will spare the region of Goshen, where my people live. No flies will be found there. Then you will know that I am the Lord and that I am present even in the heart of your land. I will make a clear distinction between my people and your people."

Reflection:

This is what God told Pharaoh before he sent a plague of flies to Egypt. Even today, God lives in the heart of our land and is able to punish the wicked while blessing the godly. Some other ways that God punishes is with fire, natural disasters, famine, and disease. His children have no need to worry because God, our Father, is faithful to take care of us no matter what may be happening in the world.

EXODUS 9

Passage: "Pharaoh again became stubborn. Because his heart was hard, Pharaoh refused to let the people leave, just as the Lord had predicted through Moses."

Reflection:

A plague killed all the livestock in Egypt, followed by a plague of festering boils on the people and animals, and then a devastating hailstorm that killed people, animals, plants, and trees. Even after these events, Pharaoh would not let the Israelites leave Egypt because his heart was hard and stubborn. Do you know someone like that? These are people who refuse to turn to God for help even though they are struggling and suffering. Sometimes it takes a long time or something life-threatening for proud and stubborn people to turn to God for salvation. However, during all these plagues in Egypt, who was safe and sound? The Israelites, their animals, and their property in the land of Goshen.

God said to Pharaoh, "By now I could have lifted my hand and struck you and your people with a plague to wipe you off the face of the earth. But I have spared you for a purpose—to show you my power and to spread my fame throughout the earth." God has a good purpose for everything. We may not fully understand what it is at the time, which is why we must trust him and be thankful we belong to him.

EXODUS 10

Passage: "This is what the Lord, the God of the Hebrews says: "'How long will you refuse to submit to me?'"

Reflection:

As God continued to do his miracles, which became more painful, Pharaoh began to soften. Prior to the plague of locusts, Pharaoh said that he would never allow the Israelites to take their children with them to worship the Lord. God's reply was "Bring on the locusts!"

After the next plague of complete darkness for three days in Egypt, except for where the people of Israel lived, Pharaoh said, "Go and worship the Lord. You may even take your little ones with you…but not your livestock." Pharaoh was gradually giving in to the demands of the Lord, but he was still holding out from complete submission. God had a plan for that in Pharaoh's life, in your life, and in my life.

EXODUS 11

Passage: "Then the Lord said to Moses, 'I will strike Pharaoh and the land of Egypt with one more blow. After that, Pharaoh will let you leave this country. In fact, he will be so eager to get rid of you he will force you all to leave.'"

Reflection:

Since Pharaoh still had not obeyed God and let the people of Israel leave Egypt, God was going to strike them with one more blow. Moses warned Pharaoh of what was going to happen: all the firstborn sons were going to die at midnight that night. Did Pharaoh let the Israelites leave before this happened? No! You can warn people repeatedly of the consequences of their actions, but sometimes they are just too stubborn to listen.

God was still taking care of the Israelites and getting them ready to leave Egypt. He told Moses to tell them to ask their Egyptian neighbors for silver and gold. God also said that during the night of this final blow to Egypt's firstborn sons, there would be wailing throughout the land of Egypt like no one had heard before or would hear again. It would be so peaceful for the Israelites that not even a dog would bark. The Lord was again going to make a distinction between those who belonged to him and those who did not.

EXODUS 12

Passage: "For the Lord will pass through the land to strike down the Egyptians. But when he sees the blood on the top and sides of the doorframe, the Lord will pass over your home. He will not permit his death angel to enter your house and strike you down."

Reflection:

Jesus is our Passover lamb. God told the Israelites to choose a male lamb (or goat) with no defects for a sacrifice. Having never sinned, Jesus is our sacrifice without defects. The Israelites were to smear the blood of the lamb on the top and sides of the doors of their houses. The blood of Jesus is the door of salvation for everyone, the only door to God and eternal life and Heaven. When we accept Jesus, the only sacrifice for sin, as our Savior, God sees that we are covered through faith on the doors of our hearts by the blood of Jesus, so the plague of death and Hell will not touch us.

Like the Egyptians who were not covered by the blood of the lamb on their doors, God will execute judgment and strike down those who are not covered by the blood of Jesus. This will happen on the last day when time runs out at midnight.

Like no outsiders and no uncircumcised male could

celebrate the Lord's Passover, no unsaved people will be allowed to celebrate in Heaven. When we put our faith in Jesus Christ, our hearts are circumcised. God accepts us as his children and declares us righteous because of our faith. The Lord kept his promise to bring the Israelites out of Egypt and, in the end, he will keep his promise to bring his children into the kingdom.

EXODUS 13

Passage: "And in the future, your children will ask you, 'What does all this mean?' Then you will tell them, 'With the power of his mighty hand, the Lord brought us out of Egypt, the place of our slavery.'"

Reflection:

We, as Christians, can compare our past lives of slavery to sin to the Israelites' slavery in Egypt. Egypt is where we lived, in sin, before Christ. However, God rescued us and set us free from our Egypt with the power of his mighty hand. God wants us to remember, share, and celebrate what he did for us.

When we accept Jesus as our Savior and Lord, God doesn't usually take us immediately to Heaven, the Promised Land. Instead of taking the shortest route, he leads us in a roundabout way through the wilderness of life on earth, just like he did with the Israelites. To do this, we must be like soldiers in God's army, ready for battle every day.

Be assured, God will never remove his presence from us. He goes ahead of us, he guides us, and he provides us with his light, day and night.

EXODUS 14

Passage: "Don't be afraid. Just stand still and watch the Lord rescue you today. The Egyptians you see today will never be seen again. The Lord himself will fight for you. Just stay calm."

Reflection:

If the angel of the Lord moved between God's people and their enemies and kept them from approaching each other all night, then God can certainly protect us from our enemies. If God opened a path so his people could walk through the sea on dry ground with walls of water on each side, then God can make a path through any impossible situation.

God was fighting for the Israelites, and the Egyptians knew it. When God unleashed his mighty power against the enemies of his people, it filled them with awe and strengthened their faith in him. God plans events, sometimes scary events, to display his glory and so people will know that he is Lord.

EXODUS 15

Passage: "The Lord is a warrior. Yahweh is his name! The Lord hurled both horse and rider into the sea. He is glorious in power. His right hand smashes the enemy. He overthrows those who rise against him. He unleashes his blazing fury and consumes them like straw."

Reflection:

God demonstrates his unfailing love for the redeemed by protecting them from their enemies. After being delivered by God from Egypt and watching him drown Pharaoh and his army in the Red Sea, the Israelites praised God with song. Even today, God still fights for his people. We should be thankful by worshiping and singing to God like the Israelites did.

Three days after this great deliverance, the Israelites couldn't find water, then the water they did find was bitter. What did they do? Pray to God for help? No, they complained and turned against Moses. Moses prayed to God, and he miraculously made the bitter water turn good. How quickly we, like the Israelites, forget about God's great love and power.

EXODUS 16

Passage: "Look, I'm going to rain down food from heaven for you. Each day the people can go out and pick up as much food as they need for the day. I will test them in this to see whether or not they will follow my instructions."

Reflection:

Manna, bread from Heaven, can be likened to Jesus, the true Bread from Heaven. When we accept him into our hearts, he fills us up with his sacred Holy Spirit and gives us the grace we need for each day.

As it was with the Israelites, it is today: "some of them didn't listen" to the Lord's instructions. Some people don't believe God, they doubt his Word, and they don't have faith in him or his promises. As Christians, let us have strong faith, listen to and obey God, and trust that he will always provide for all our needs and keep every promise in his Holy Bible.

EXODUS 17

Passage: "Strike the rock, and water will come gushing out. Then the people will be able to drink."

Reflection:

The Israelites drank from the spiritual rock that traveled with them, and that rock was Christ. Anyone who asks Jesus into his or her heart will be filled with the living water of the Holy Spirit, which becomes a fresh, bubbling spring within that person, giving him or her eternal life. The person will never be thirsty again.

With Aaron and Hur holding up Moses's arm with the staff in his hand, the Lord gave Joshua victory over the Amalekites. Likewise, we should encourage the exhausted and strengthen the weak—especially our brothers and sisters in Christ—so they can endure and have victory in their battles.

EXODUS 18

Passage: "If you follow this advice, and if God commands you to do so, then you will be able to endure the pressures, and all these people will go home in peace."

Reflection:

"The righteous person faces many troubles, but the Lord comes to the rescue each time." Here we see an example of this truth. Moses was telling Jethro, his father-in-law, about all the good things the Lord had done for Israel and how he rescued them from the Egyptians and all their troubles. Jethro was very encouraged and praised God. As we share what God has done for us with others, it strengthens and encourages both them and us.

Jethro offered Moses some good advice, which he followed, about how to share the workload with others so Moses wouldn't wear himself out trying to do everything. He also told Moses to continue to represent the people before God (like Jesus does for believers), teach them God's decrees, give them his instructions, and show them how to conduct their lives.

God gives us Jesus, the Holy Spirit, and the Bible to help us today, but sometimes he sends godly people into our lives to help us. If the advice they give points to God, then we can consider following their suggestions.

EXODUS 19

Passage: "Now if you will obey me and keep my covenant, you will be my own special treasure from among all the peoples on earth; for all the earth belongs to me."

Reflection:

If God asked you if you would like to be his own special treasure, what would you say? I'd say, "Yes!" God says that if we are his children, through Jesus Christ, and obey him, then we are his own special treasures from among all the people of the earth. What a blessing to be thought of by our Father in this way!

What does God want to do with his people? He wants to speak to us, like he did with the Israelites. God wants to come to us, he wants us to hear him speak, and he wants to have fellowship with us. God may or may not appear to us in the form of fire on the top of a mountain. God can reveal himself to you in any way he chooses: in roaring thunder, flashing lightening, a dense cloud, or in a violently shaking mountain. Prepare for his arrival, consecrate yourself to him, and be ready to hear from God.

EXODUS 20

Passage: "Then God gave the people all these instructions."

Reflection:

The Ten Commandments that God gave to the people can be simplified into two commands: love God and love others.

The first four commandments are about loving God. You must not have any other gods or idols of any king, must not misuse God's name, and must keep the seventh day as a holy day of rest dedicated to the Lord.

The remaining six commandments are about loving others. Honor your father and mother, don't murder, don't commit adultery, don't steal, don't testify falsely against others, and don't covet what belongs to others.

The Ten Commandments are about one thing: *love.*

EXODUS 21

Passage: "But if there is further injury, the punishment must match the injury: a life for a life, an eye for an eye, a tooth for a tooth, a hand for a hand, a foot for a foot, a burn for a burn, a wound for a wound, a bruise for a bruise."

Reflection:

God loves fair and just treatment. Some of the things he says in his Word include the following.

"For I, the Lord, love justice."

"For the Lord loves justice, and he will never abandon the godly."

"Don't be misled—you cannot mock the justice of God. You will always harvest what you plant."

"He will judge the world with justice and rule the nations with fairness."

"For the righteous Lord loves justice, the virtuous will see his face."

"At the time I have planned, I will bring justice against the wicked."

"The Lord gives righteousness and justice to all who are treated unfairly."

"It is not right to acquit the guilty or deny justice to the innocent."

"If they twist justice in the courts—doesn't the Lord see all these things?"

"God blesses those who hunger and thirst for justice, for they will be satisfied."

"In his justice, he will pay back those who persecute you."

"Don't worry, judgment and justice will be upheld."

EXODUS 22

Passage: "You must not dishonor God or curse any of your rulers."

Reflection:

This is another example of love for God and love for others. If we love God, we will not dishonor him and if we love others, we will not curse them. God puts all people with authority in their positions for a purpose, and God removes them when it's time. We should respect God's decision even though we may not agree or understand.

We may think that we are in control of elections or appointments to positions of any kind, but we are not. God steers the hearts of people to accomplish his divine will, which will culminate with the events in Revelation when everyone stands before the One appointed by God. "And Jesus is the one appointed by God to be the judge of all—the living and the dead."

EXODUS 23

Passage: "I will drive them out a little at a time."

Reflection:

God says, "You must not follow the crowd in doing wrong." When the world, or even the law, says it's acceptable to do something that is morally wrong, Christians must obey the Word of God.

God says, "See, I am sending you an angel before you to protect you on your journey and lead you safely to the place I have prepared for you." Believers have divine protection by angels too. The Lord Jesus, through the Holy Spirit, leads us on our journeys until we get to Heaven, the place God has prepared for us.

God says, "Follow my instructions, then I will be an enemy to your enemies, and I will oppose those who oppose you." If we obey our Father, he is on our side and will bless us.

How does God work? A little at a time. When God works, it appears that things just happen naturally over time. People don't often think about the fact that God is in control of everything. When you pray, wait and watch God work in your situation a little at a time.

EXODUS 24

Passage: "Then the Lord instructed Moses: 'Come up here to me.'"

Reflection:

Unlike during the days of Moses, who was the only one allowed to come near to the Lord, all believers today can come near to the Lord through the Holy Spirit and prayer. However, the key to coming near to God is still the same: obedience.

After Moses had written down all the Lord's instructions in the Book of the Covenant and read it to the people, they all agreed to obey everything. Then Moses took some blood from the animals offered to God and splattered it over the people. This pictures the future death and shedding of blood of the Messiah, Jesus. Those who accept Jesus by faith are forever covered and purified with his blood. Without the shedding of blood, there is no forgiveness of sin.

EXODUS 25

Passage: "The Lord said to Moses, 'Tell the people of Israel to bring me their sacred offerings. Accept the contributions from all those whose hearts are moved to offer them.'"

Reflection:

Just as God moved the hearts of people to make sacred offerings for the Tabernacle, the Holy Spirit moves the hearts of people to accept Jesus as their Savior and give him the sacred offering of their surrendered lives.

The Ark's cover, the place of atonement, was a holy place made of pure gold. Jesus's blood provides us with cleansing, forgiveness, and reconciliation to God. His blood covers our sins and provides atonement.

The Bread of the Presence is also representative of Jesus, as he is the Bread that came down from Heaven. Jesus is with us at all times, just as Moses was instructed by God to have the bread on the table at all times.

The lampstand represents the light that Jesus provides for his followers. Always reflecting his light forward, Jesus shows us the way we should go.

EXODUS 26

Passage: "Make the Tabernacle from ten curtains of finely woven linen. Decorate the curtains with blue, purple, and scarlet thread and with skillfully embroidered cherubim."

Reflection:

God gave very detailed instructions to Moses about how to construct the Tabernacle, with exact measurements and design details. God was very particular about this place of worship, and he hasn't changed. Congregations should give as much care and attention to detail to churches today as churches reflect their love for God and honor him.

EXODUS 27

Passage: "Command the people of Israel to bring you pure oil of pressed olives for the light, to keep the lamps burning continually."

Reflection:

The light for the Tabernacle of God was fueled by oil and was to be kept burning. When we receive the Holy Spirit through salvation, our bodies become Tabernacles of God. The oil of the Holy Spirit produces the light that continually burns in believers. Some may have bright lights, and some may have dim lights, depending on their level of submission to God. However, the light will never go out.

EXODUS 28

Passage: "Call for your brother, Aaron, and his sons, Nadab, Abihu, Eleazar, and Ithamar. Set them apart from the rest of the people of Israel so they may minister to me and be my priests."

Reflection:

Like Aaron and his sons, who were set apart from the people for service to God, we are set apart for God by faith in Jesus Christ. Believers are a chosen people, royal priests, and holy. We are God's very own possessions who he called out of darkness into his wonderful light.

Aaron carried the objects used to determine the Lord's will over his heart, but Christians today have the Holy Spirit of God living in their hearts, and he tells us the will of God.

Aaron was to wear a medallion of pure gold with the words "Holy to the Lord" attached to the front of his turban so he could take on himself any guilt of the people. Jesus is our perfect high priest forever: holy, blameless, and unstained by sin. When he died on the cross, he took on himself the guilt from all sin for all people. Jesus has been given the highest place of honor and he is always in the presence of God the Father in the holiest of holy places, Heaven.

EXODUS 29

Passage: "Each day, offer two lambs that are a year old, one in the morning and the other in the evening."

Reflection:

Anointing with oil, as done with Aaron and his sons, can be compared to being anointed with the Holy Spirit when we accept Jesus as our Savior. Believers become holy in the eyes of God when this happens.

Aaron was to make sacrifices to God each morning and evening which consisted of a lamb (Jesus is the Lamb of God), flour (the body of Christ), and wine (the blood of Christ).

Likewise, after we are anointed with the Holy Spirit, we should give our time to spend with Jesus in the morning and evening. This is a pleasing offering to the Lord.

EXODUS 30

Passage: "Each man who is counted must pay a ransom for himself to the Lord...This offering is given to the Lord to purify your lives, making you right with him."

Reflection:

Who does this sound like? Jesus! Jesus paid a ransom for each of us with his own blood, not mere money. His blood purifies us, making us right with God forever, if we accept him as our Savior. When we do, we are clean because our sin is washed away (washbasin) and we are anointed with the Holy Spirit (anointing oil). We become pure, holy, and reserved for the Lord. Our godly lives are a sweet-smelling fragrance to him, like incense.

EXODUS 31

Passage: "You must keep the Sabbath day, for it is a holy day for you."

Reflection:

Just as God specifically chose Bezalel and Oholiab to make the Tabernacle and everything in it, we are chosen by God specifically for certain jobs. God filled those men with the Holy Spirit and gave them great wisdom, ability, and expertise in all kinds of crafts. He enabled them to do the jobs that they were created for. The Holy Spirit also gives us special gifts and skills so that we can do what God planned for us, even before we were born.

The Sabbath day is a holy day. God tells us not to work but to rest on that day. It's a day to remember the future and current rest we have in Christ as his children—we are "human beings" not human "doings." God rested and was refreshed on the seventh day after creating the heavens and the earth in six days. Likewise, we are to rest on the seventh day and trust God to take care of us. Resting from work one day each week is as much a part of bearing God's image as doing work.

EXODUS 32

Passage: "When the people saw how long it was taking Moses to come back down the mountain, they gathered around Aaron. 'Come on,' they said, 'make us some gods who can lead us. We don't know what happened to this fellow Moses, who brought us here from the land of Egypt.'"

Reflection:

While Moses was on the mountain with God for forty days and nights, the people became impatient and asked Aaron to "make us some gods who can lead us." Aaron should have said no and reminded them of their covenant with the one and only God. Instead, he told them to bring their gold rings to him and he made them a calf idol. Later he lied to Moses and said, "I simply threw it into the fire and out came this calf." Aaron let the people get completely out of control.

This whole mess started with impatience. The people tried to take matters into their own hands. Weak leadership was thrown into the mix and out popped idol worship. Idol worship angered God, which led to the slaying of 3,000 people and a plague for the remaining Israelites.

EXODUS 33

Passage: "If it is true that you look favorably on me, let me know your ways so I may understand you more fully and continue to enjoy your favor."

Reflection:

This should be our pursuit and request of God too: a deeper understanding of him and his ways. The Lord replied, "I will personally go with you, Moses, and I will give you rest—everything will be fine for you." As obedient children of God, this is true for us. God never leaves us and as we trust in him, he gives us rest.

"For your presence among us sets your people and me apart from all other people on the earth." This is still true. People are either God's children by faith in Jesus Christ or they are not. They are either God's friends or his enemies. They are either saved or unsaved. The Holy Spirit either lives in them or he doesn't. Those who belong to God are set apart by him from those who do not.

God said to Moses, "I will indeed do what you have asked, for I look favorably on you, and I know you by name." God knows us by name too. He created us, chose us to belong to him, and looks favorably on his children. He is a loving Father. Don't be afraid to ask him for what you want, big or small, because he just might give you what you ask for, or something even better.

EXODUS 34

Passage: "Then the Lord said to Moses, 'Chisel out two stone tablets like the first ones. I will write on them the same words that were on the tablets you smashed.'"

Reflection:

God was so kind and patient with Moses after he smashed the first stone tablets. God told Moses to make two new tablets, and he rewrote everything that was in the first set again on the second set. Even when we mess up, our Father gives us do-overs.

Our God, Yahweh, is full of compassion, mercy, unfailing love, and faithfulness. He is slow to anger, and he forgives iniquity, rebellion, and sin. However, he does not excuse the guilty and he is jealous about his relationship with us. When we are faithful and obedient to our Father, putting him first in our love and in our lives, we will be blessed.

Moses had a radiant glow on his face whenever he spoke to the Lord. The more time we spend with God in his Word, the more we become like him on the inside and on the outside.

EXODUS 35

Passage: "Both men and women came, all whose hearts were willing. They brought to the Lord their offerings."

Reflection:

The Lord commanded Moses to take a sacred offering to build the Tabernacle. Among the items requested were gold, silver, gemstones, and wood. These things were given out of generosity from the willing hearts of men and women whose spirits were moved by God. These items can be compared to the value of a believer's works, done with a willing heart for God.

The works that Jesus judges as being more valuable will receive higher rewards in Heaven. This tells us that not all believers will have the same level of experience in Heaven; it depends on what they do for God on earth. No one can lay any foundation other than the one we already have: Jesus Christ. Anyone who builds on that foundation may use a variety of materials: gold, silver, jewels, wood, hay, or straw. However, on the judgment day, fire will reveal what kind of work each builder has done. The fire will show if a person's work has any value. If the work survives, the builder will receive a reward. If the work is burned up, the builder will suffer great loss. The builder will be saved, but like someone barely escaping through a wall of flames.

EXODUS 36

Passage: "The people have given more than enough materials to complete the job the Lord has commanded us to do."

Reflection:

When God tells his children to do something, he will always supply whatever they need to do it—sometimes more than enough. Don't worry about not having enough time, money, energy, skill, or wisdom to complete the things that God is telling you to do. Just do them. God is trustworthy and faithful in supplying you with more than enough.

EXODUS 37

Passage: "Next Bezalel made the Ark of acacia wood—a sacred chest...he overlaid it inside and outside with pure gold."

Reflection:

The Ark of the Covenant that Bezalel built was a copy of the real one in Heaven. God gave Moses the pattern when they met on the mountain. In the book of Revelation we read, "Then, in Heaven, the Temple of God was opened and the Ark of his covenant could be seen inside the Temple. Lightning flashed, thunder crashed and roared, and there was an earthquake and a terrible hailstorm." How awesome that God has given us a glimpse of Heaven on earth.

Reading:

EXODUS 38

Passage: "Bezalel son of Uri, grandson of Hur, of the
tribe of Judah, made everything just as the
Lord had commanded Moses."

Reflection:

Bezalel was chosen by God to make the Tabernacle
and its furnishings. We can see that he was obedient,
detail-oriented, creative, gifted, patient, and talented as
well as a perfectionist and a leader. What an honor to
be chosen by God to serve him in this way. Without the
assistance of Oholiab and the people who donated all the
supplies, Bezalel would not have been able to succeed.
God stirred the hearts of the Israelites to give and work
together. God was the divine project manager leading
this sacred construction project.

EXODUS 39

Passage: "So the people of Israel followed all of the Lord's instructions to Moses. Then Moses inspected all their work. When he found it had been done as the Lord had commanded him, he blessed them."

Reflection:

This was the first tabernacle ever built. It was important for the people of Israel to have a place where they could go to worship God. It is still important for Christians to regularly worship God in church with their forever families. It's a picture of what worship will be like in Heaven.

God commanded that the Tabernacle be built to his exact specifications, and when the people obeyed, they were blessed. Do you want God to lavish you with his unfailing love and blessings? Then show your love for God by obeying him.

EXODUS 40

Passage: "The cloud of the Lord hovered over the Tabernacle during the day, and at night fire glowed inside the cloud so the whole family of Israel could see it. This continued throughout all their journeys."

Reflection:

How secure the Israelites must have felt when they were able to see the cloud of the Lord with them day and night. When the cloud lifted from the Tabernacle, the people would follow it and continue their journey. Although we don't have a cloud to lead us through life, believers do have the indwelling Holy Spirit who leads them day and night. The Holy Spirit is the light inside our bodily Tabernacles. We are secure because we belong to God and we are always in his presence.

✧ ✧ ✧

LAW BOOK 3

Leviticus

LEVITICUS 1

Passage: "Lay your hand on the animal's head, and the Lord will accept its death in your place to purify you, making you right with him."

Reflection:

The burnt offering was a special gift that pleased the Lord. The sacrificed animal was to be a male with no defects. The Lord accepted its death in place of the person's death. The offering purified the person making the sacrifice and made the person right with God.

Since Jesus came down from Heaven and died on the cross as the perfect, sinless Son of God, there is no longer a need for animal sacrifices. Jesus died in our place. He was our sacrifice to God, so those who believe and accept him as their Savior will not die because of their sins. Jesus's offering of himself purifies us and makes us right with God.

LEVITICUS 2

Passage: "When you present grain as an offering to the Lord, the offering must consist of choice flour."

Reflection:

The grain offered to God consisted of choice flour, olive oil, and frankincense. It contained no yeast and was seasoned with salt. It was most holy and offered on the altar.

The grain offering symbolizes Jesus. He is the choicest bread who came down from Heaven. He is our High Priest (frankincense). He was sinless (no yeast). By accepting Jesus, we are anointed with the Holy Spirit of God (olive oil), become the salt of the earth, and receive the blessings of God's eternal covenant. Jesus was most holy. He was offered to God on the altar of the cross.

LEVITICUS 3

Passage: "If you present an animal from the herd as a peace offering to the Lord, it may be a male or a female, but it must have no defects."

Reflection:

The Israelites made peace offerings to God. Instead of sacrificing an animal, the message of Good News for the people of Israel, and all people, is that there is peace with God through Jesus Christ, who is Lord of all.

Jesus is our peace offering. He gives us peace with God and the peace of God. He guides us to the path of peace when we believe in him. Jesus said, "I am leaving you with a gift—peace of mind and heart. And the peace I give is a gift the world cannot give. So don't be troubled or afraid."

LEVITICUS 4

Passage: "The Lord said to Moses, 'Give the following instructions to the people of Israel. This is how you are to deal with those who sin unintentionally by doing anything that violates one of the Lord's commands.'"

Reflection:

If someone sins by violating one of the Lord's commands but he or she does not realize it, the person is still guilty. This point is emphasized three times in this chapter, and it is still true today. The difference is that the Israelites had to offer animal sacrifices for their sins, but the blood of Christ continually cleanses believers, forgiving us and making us right with God.

Notice also the different animals required for the sins of the high priest, the entire community, a leader, and a common person. The sacrifice appears to go from higher value for the high priest to low value for the common person. This shows that God holds people who are in positions of authority, especially church leaders, more accountable to obey his Word than the common person.

LEVITICUS 5

Passage: "When you become aware of your guilt in any of these ways, you must confess your sin."

Reflection:

When we sin, intentionally or unintentionally, we are guilty before the Lord. If the Israelites presented a sin offering or a guilt offering to God, they would be forgiven, purified, and made right with the Lord.

Jesus paid for our sins, past, present, and future, on the cross. We can never lose our salvation. However, sin can interfere with our fellowship with God, so believers need to confess and turn from their sins to restore and maintain close fellowship with him.

LEVITICUS 6

Passage: "In each generation, the high priest who succeeds Aaron must prepare the same offering. It belongs to the Lord and must be burned up completely."

Reflection:

Aaron and his male descendants could eat from the special gifts offered to the Lord at the Temple. Today, those who preach should be supported from the offerings of those who benefit from their preaching.

The grain offering made to the Lord when Aaron and his sons were anointed as priests was to be burned up entirely. None of it was to be eaten. This illustrates the life of a servant who is entirely devoted to God. As the person's life is used up in service to God, nothing is leftover.

LEVITICUS 7

Passage: "You must never eat fat, whether from cattle, sheep, or goats...Anyone who consumes blood will be cut off from the community...Any meat left over until the third day must be completely burned up."

Reflection:

Consuming fat or blood was forbidden by God for the people of Israel. It makes healthy sense that we should not eat animal fat or blood either. In addition, don't keep leftovers too long or they will be contaminated, and you will become sick if you eat them. This was a sin for the Israelites, but God was protecting them from food poisoning too.

LEVITICUS 8

Passage: "He placed the turban on Aaron's head and attached the gold medallion—the badge of holiness—to the front of the turban just as the Lord had commanded him."

Reflection:

Moses truly loved God. We know this because he obeyed God. Five times in this chapter, we read the phrase "just as the Lord had commanded him." Jesus said, "Those who accept my commandments and obey them are the ones who love me." Obedience is the true measure of our love for God.

The Lord commanded the process of ordination to purify Aaron and his sons, making them right with God. If they failed to stay at the entrance of the Tabernacle day and night for seven days and do everything the Lord required, they would die. Aaron and his sons also obeyed the Lord and did everything he commanded through Moses.

Thank God for his love and the gift of salvation and eternal life through Jesus. Because of God's grace, we are forever secure as his children. We will not experience spiritual death, even when we fail to do everything God commands. When Jesus is your Lord and Savior, there is no fear of condemnation or death.

LEVITICUS 9

Passage: "Present all these offerings to the Lord because the Lord will appear to you today… and the glory of the Lord appeared to the whole community. Fire blazed forth from the Lord's presence and consumed the burnt offering and the fat on the altar. When the people saw this, they shouted with joy and fell face down to the ground."

Reflection:

What if you were told that the Lord would appear to you today? Would you be excited, happy, or scared? The Lord may not appear suddenly in a dramatic way as he did for the Israelites, but he does reveal his presence to everyone through creation. The sunshine, the birds, the trees, and flowers all reveal God's presence to everyone.

For believers who have been made pure by the blood of Jesus and are aware of the indwelling Holy Spirit, God can reveal himself in ways that many people would not perceive. God is all around us and he does reveal himself in ways that might surprise us. Thank God and present him with your offering of worship by spending time with him in his Word and prayer each day.

LEVITICUS 10

Passage: "So fire blazed forth from the Lord's presence and burned them up, and they died there before the Lord."

Reflection:

God is entirely holy. When he commanded the priests to do things a specific way in the Tabernacle, he was to be obeyed. However, Aaron's sons Nahab and Abihu, whether intentionally or unintentionally, disobeyed God by burning the wrong kind of fire.

When God tells us to do or not do something, it's for our own good. We should be careful to obey him and not become upset if we are disciplined for doing wrong. Thank God for his grace, mercy, and forgiveness through Jesus. Because of Jesus, we are free and no longer live under the law of Moses. What a relief! There are only two main things that we need to remember: love God and love others.

LEVITICUS 11

Passage: "By these instructions you will know what is unclean and clean, and which animals may be eaten and which may not be eaten."

Reflection:

God, being the good Father that he is, even taught the people of Israel about which animals they could eat, and which ones were off limits. Under the law, eating an animal that was considered detestable defiled a person's body and made him or her temporarily unclean.

Under grace, Jesus said, "It's not what goes into your mouth that defiles you; you are defiled by the words that come out of your mouth...But the words you speak come from the heart—that's what defiles you."

LEVITICUS 12

Passage: "When the time of purification is completed for either a son or a daughter, the woman must bring a one-year-old lamb for a burnt offering and a young pigeon or turtle dove for a purification offering.

Reflection:

Thirty-three days after the birth of a son, a woman must bring to the Tabernacle a one-year-old lamb for a burnt offering and a pigeon or turtle dove for a purification offering. If she cannot afford to bring a lamb, she can substitute a turtle dove or a pigeon for the burnt offering.

Mary did not take a lamb for the burnt offering, but she did take Jesus, the Lamb of God, to the Tabernacle to dedicate him to the Lord thirty-three days after his birth. Thirty-three years later, Jesus would be a purification offering for all people.

LEVITICUS 13

Passage: "Those who suffer from a serious skin disease must tear their clothing and leave their hair uncombed. They must cover their mouth and call out, 'Unclean! Unclean!' As long as the serious disease lasts, they will be ceremonially unclean. They must live in isolation in their place outside the camp."

Reflection:

Although this refers to a serious skin disease, it also applies to sin. Sin is a problem that is more than skin-deep; it is serious. The person is defiled and unclean.

A person living in sin should live as a person in mourning because he or she is not allowed into the Kingdom of God. As wool, linen, or leather items contaminated with serious mildew must be burned, the person living in sin without Jesus will be completely destroyed by fire. However, Jesus's blood cleanses those who accept him as Savior and brings them forever into the Kingdom of God.

Even after we are saved, God knows that we are still human, not perfect like him. He tells us in the Bible that if we confess our sins to him, he is faithful and just to forgive us of our sins and to cleanse us from all wickedness. God wants us to regularly confess our sins to him not to keep our salvation (because once we are saved, we are always saved) but to keep close fellowship with him and live inside the camp.

LEVITICUS 14

Passage: "And the Lord said to Moses, 'The following instructions are for those seeking ceremonial purification from a skin disease.'"

Reflection:

The ceremony for a person seeking purification from a skin disease included a stick of cedar, scarlet yarn, and a hyssop branch. These items foreshadow the death of Jesus Christ, the Messiah. The cedar stick is the cross, the scarlet yarn is his blood, and the hyssop branch was used to lift a sponge soaked with wine to Jesus's lips as he hung on the cross.

When a person had a healed skin disease, he or she had to make a guilt offering and a sin offering to the Lord. The priest would also apply olive oil to the person. These actions would purify a person and the person would be ceremonially clean before the Lord. These offerings picture what happens when a person accepts Jesus as his or her Savior. His blood removes our guilt and sin. The Holy Spirit indwells us. We are purified and clean children of God.

LEVITICUS 15

Passage: "For their impurity would defile my Tabernacle."

Reflection:

When a person had a bodily discharge, he or she was considered impure, and the person's uncleanness would defile the Tabernacle. If the person did not follow the law to become ceremonially clean, he or she would die.

In the New Testament, we read about a woman who suffered with constant bleeding for twelve years. She had spent everything she had to pay doctors, but her condition had worsened. She had faith that if she could touch the fringe of Jesus's robe, she would be healed. She touched Jesus's robe, and she was healed that moment. Jesus said, "Daughter, be encouraged! Your faith has made you well. Go in peace. Your suffering is over." The woman's faith in Jesus healed her, not the fact that she touched his robe.

Salvation works the same way. When we put our faith in Jesus and ask him to forgive our sins and cleanse us, we are saved that moment. We are forgiven and our name is written in permanent ink in the Lamb's Book of Life. Without salvation, we would die for our impurities.

LEVITICUS 16

Passage: "The Lord said to Moses, 'Warn your brother Aaron not to enter the Most Holy Place behind the inner curtain whenever he chooses; if he does, he will die. For the Ark's cover—the place of atonement—is there, and I myself am present in the cloud above the atonement cover.'"

Reflection:

At the moment when Jesus died on the cross, the curtain in the sanctuary of the Temple was torn in two from top to bottom by God. Jesus's sacrifice allows us to enter into God's presence freely. His door is always open to us.

"The bull and the goat presented as sin offerings, whose blood Aaron takes into the Most Holy Place for the purification ceremony, will be carried outside the camp." Jesus also suffered and died outside the city gates to make his people holy by means of his own blood.

"This is a permanent law for you, to purify the people of Israel from their sins, making them right with the Lord once each year." Unlike the priest on earth who entered the Most Holy Place year after year to atone for sin with the blood of an animal, Christ did not need to die again and again. His one-time sacrifice, to remove sin by his own death, was good for all time, past, present, and future. Now, Jesus is in Heaven appearing before God the Father on our behalf.

LEVITICUS 17

Passage: "I have given you the blood on the altar to purify you, making you right with the Lord."

Reflection:

You cannot worship the Lord and demons too. If the Israelites sacrificed a bull, lamb, or goat in a field to the demons instead of bringing it to the Tabernacle as an offering to the Lord, they were as guilty as murderers and were to be cut off from the community. We, as believers who belong to the Kingdom of God, are blessed when we are faithful to the Lord in all things.

The life of any creature is in its blood. Blood given in exchange for a life makes purification possible. The blood of animals on the altar was used to purify the Israelites. Later Jesus, the Messiah, gave his blood on the cross as a permanent sacrifice to purify all people who accept and believe in him. God made Christ, who never sinned, to be the offering for our sin, so that we could be made right with God through Christ.

LEVITICUS 18

Passage: "You must obey all my regulations and be careful to obey my decrees, for I am the Lord your God. If you obey my decrees and my regulations, you will find life through them. I am the Lord."

Reflection:

God said not to practice any of these detestable activities. Do not have sexual relations with a close relative. Do not have sexual relations with a neighbor's wife. Do not have sexual relations with a woman during her period of menstrual impurity. Do not permit any of your children to be offered as sacrifices. Do not practice homosexuality, having sex with another man as with a woman. Do not have sex with an animal.

These sins defile people and the land where they live. Do not act like unbelievers or imitate their sinful way of life. We find new life by obeying God. As God punished the people then, causing the land to vomit them out, he still punishes people today for sin.

LEVITICUS 19

Passage: "You must be holy because I, the Lord your God, am holy."

Reflection:

Like the Lord our God, we should be holy, pure, and honest in our character, conduct, and conversation. We are to love, obey, and trust God and love others as we love ourselves. God tells us to be respectful of others, not insulting. We are not to spread slanderous gossip, seek revenge, hold grudges, or take advantage of others.

LEVITICUS 20

Passage: "And if the people of the community ignore those who offer their children to Molech and refuse to execute them, I myself will turn against them and their families and will cut them off from the community...If a man practices homosexuality, having sex with another man as with a woman, both men have committed a detestable act. They must both be put to death, for they are guilty of a capital offense."

Reflection:

Sin creates a barrier in our fellowship with our holy heavenly Father. The punishment for any and all sin is eternal death. However, Jesus took the punishment for all who believe in him, so we will not experience spiritual death, but will have eternal life.

God sees everything and he will punish people for sin, so don't think that you or others will get away with it. Don't be misled: you cannot mock the justice of God. You will always harvest what you plant. Those who live only to satisfy their own sinful natures will harvest decay and death. However, those who live to please God will harvest everlasting life from the Spirit.

LEVITICUS 21

Passage: "They (priests) must be set apart as holy to their God and must never bring shame on the name of God."

Reflection:

God is holy. Jesus is our holy High Priest. When we receive salvation through Jesus, we become holy priests too. We are indwelled by the Holy Spirit. In addition, we are part of a Kingdom of holy, royal priests who are set apart for God. God is holy and he makes those who belong to him holy too.

LEVITICUS 22

Passage: "It was I who rescued you from the land of Egypt, that I might be your God. I am the Lord."

Reflection:

Like he did with the Israelites, God sees our oppression and hears our groans. Jesus came down from Heaven to rescue us from the evil one, so he could be our God and we could serve him without fear and help rescue others. God rescued us from death and the terrors of the coming judgment. He transferred us from Egypt, the kingdom of darkness, into the Kingdom of God.

LEVITICUS 23

Passage: "This is a permanent law for you, and it must be observed from generation to generation wherever you live."

Reflection:

In addition to the weekly Lord's Sabbath Day, God appointed annual festivals: official holy days of assembly. An event only happens once, like the birth of Jesus. After that, we celebrate to remember that important event. Remembering is important because it reminds each new generation of the event. It's also important to remember God's faithfulness in the past as we look forward to the future. God remembers all his promises, and he keeps every single one. We should also remember God in our daily lives and give him thanks in all circumstances for everything.

LEVITICUS 24

Passage: "Command the people of Israel to bring you pure oil of pressed olives for the light, to keep the lamps burning continually."

Reflection:

Jesus was pure and he was pressed continually: pressed by people, troubles, and finally crucifixion. The Holy Spirit is the pure oil of God, given to those who receive Jesus Christ as their Savior. He is the light that is continually burning in our hearts.

Blasphemy is the act of insulting or showing contempt or lack of reverence for God. The person who blasphemed the name of the Lord, under the law of Moses, was stoned to death by the community. Those who blaspheme God obviously do not know him or love him, because a person filled with the Holy Spirit will not blaspheme God. God will not blaspheme himself. God shows mercy to the ignorant. We should pray for unbelievers to understand the love of the One they curse and insult, so that they might receive his forgiveness and salvation.

LEVITICUS 25

Passage: "Be assured that I will send my blessing for you in the sixth year."

Reflection:

God says, "Show your fear of God by not taking advantage of each other. I am the Lord your God." When we live with the awareness of God's presence, it is easier to do what is right and pleasing to him.

God said, "Be assured that I will send my blessing for you in the sixth year." God always provides for his children. Even if you do not work for a year, God will take care of you and ensure that you have more than enough.

God said, "The land belongs to me. You are only foreigners and tenant farmers working for me." Everything does belong to God. We are here working for him, no matter who our employers are. We are to work enthusiastically for the Lord and pay attention to our own special work, not compare ourselves to anyone else.

God said, "I am the Lord your God, who brought you out of the land of Egypt to give you the land of Canaan and to be your God...the people of Israel are my servants." Through faith in Jesus Christ, God has brought us out of slavery to sin and death to give us freedom and eternal life in Heaven. We belong to God our Father and will serve him forever.

LEVITICUS 26

Passage: "If you follow my decrees and are careful to obey my commands…I will live among you, and I will not despise you. I will walk among you; I will be your God, and you will be my people."

Reflection:

If the Israelites obeyed God, he said that they would live securely in their own land, have peace, and sleep with no cause for fear. He said that he would look favorably upon them, giving them a surplus of crops. Best of all God said, "I will live among you; I will be your God, and you will be my people."

However, if the Israelites did not obey God, he said that he would turn against them and break their proud spirit. He would send diseases and plagues and destroy the food supply. He would devastate their land and allow their enemies to overtake them. God would despise them, demoralize them, and cause them to live in fear.

Remember, God does not change. He is the same yesterday, today, and forever. When we obey God, the result is blessings. When we disobey God, the result is punishment.

LEVITICUS 27

Passage: "One-tenth of the produce of the land, whether grain from the fields or fruit from the trees, belongs to the Lord and must be set apart to him as holy...Count off every tenth animal from your herds and flocks and set them apart for the Lord as holy."

Reflection:

One-tenth of what God gives us belongs to him. Only a small percent of Christians who give to their local churches do so through regular tithing. When we do not cheat God out of his portion, but willingly give it back to him, God said, "I will open the windows of heaven for you. I will pour out a blessing so great you won't have enough room to take it in! Try it! Put me to the test!"

✧ ✧ ✧

LAW BOOK 4

Numbers

NUMBERS 1

Passage: "The men of Israel who were twenty years
old or older were listed one by one, just as the
Lord had commanded Moses."

Reflection:

God told Moses and Aaron to register all the men
who were twenty years old or older and able to go to
war. There were 603,550 men. This did not include the
tribe of Levi, who were put in charge of the Tabernacle.
They were to set it up, take it down, and protect it from
the Israelites who might get too close to it and be put
to death by God. The book of Numbers, appropriately
named, begins with counting the troops.

NUMBERS 2

Passage: "Each clan and family set up camp and marched under their banners exactly as the Lord had instructed."

Reflection:

Everything that happened with the tribes of Israel was very organized, not haphazard. The way they set up camp and the order in which they marched was all determined by God, their Commander in Chief. In the center of everything was the Tabernacle.

Three tribes camped on the east, south, west, and north sides of the Tabernacle. The Tabernacle was surrounded by six tribes in front and six tribes behind when the tribes traveled. This is a good example of how we should live our lives in an organized manner with God at the center.

NUMBERS 3

Passage: "The Levites belong to me. I am the Lord."

Reflection:

The Levites represented about three and a half percent of the Israelite male population. They oversaw every detail related to the Tabernacle. They also took the place of the firstborn sons of the people of Israel.

What a privilege it is to belong to God through faith in Jesus Christ. Jesus redeemed us by paying for our sins, substituting his death for ours. As God's children, we are like the Levites: small, special, and set apart for service to him.

NUMBERS 4

Passage: "All the men between thirty and fifty years of age who were eligible for service in the Tabernacle and for its transportation numbered 8,580."

Reflection:

God assigned specific duties related to transporting the Tabernacle to three clans of the tribe of Levi. The Kohathite clan reported to Eleazer and were responsible for packing and carrying the sacred objects from inside the Tabernacle when they traveled. This was such an important job because they could die if they approached or looked at the sacred objects without Aaron and his sons present.

The Gershonite and Merarite clans reported to Ithamar. They were responsible for packing and carrying the exterior Tabernacle items when they traveled. The men of these three clans were between the ages of thirty and fifty. They were taught exactly how to cover and transport each item from God's house with the utmost care and respect.

God's house, whether it is the church you attend or your body that is indwelled by the Holy Spirit, deserves to be well cared for. One day we will get new eternal bodies and a new eternal home in Heaven with God.

NUMBERS 5

Passage: "If any of the people—men or women—betray the Lord by doing wrong to another person, they are guilty."

Reflection:

Since God is holy, he could not live among the Israelites with sin in the camp. The people had to be pure. They could not have skin disease, be unclean by touching a dead body, or betray the Lord by doing wrong to another person.

Jesus makes us pure by cleansing us from all sin. This allows the Holy Spirit to live in us, and it also allows us to live in Heaven, where everyone and everything is always pure and holy, with God one day. Since we are humans living in a sinful world, we will still sin on occasion. We must confess our sin to God to have close fellowship with him.

Did you ever think about the fact that doing wrong to others is betraying God? It is. When we belong to God and love him, we should want to please our Father, not betray him. Love God. Love others.

NUMBERS 6

Passage: "May the Lord bless you and protect you. May the Lord smile on you and be gracious to you. May the Lord show you his favor and give you his peace."

Reflection:

What a special blessing this is from God to his children. Every word is so wonderful and true. God gives believers his blessing and protection, his smile and his grace. The Lord also promises his favor and peace. What more could we ask for? Live in the truth of this rich blessing from the Lord every day.

NUMBERS 7

Passage: "Whenever Moses went into the Tabernacle to speak with the Lord, he heard the voice speaking to him from between the two cherubim above the Ark's cover—the place of atonement—that rests on the Ark of the Covenant. The Lord spoke to Moses from there."

Reflection:

The Lord directed Moses every step of the way. God told Moses to use the oxen and wagons to transport the Tabernacle. God told Moses to distribute them among the Levites according to the work they had to do. That is exactly what Moses did.

God still speaks to his children today. He speaks through his written Word, through his Holy Spirit, through circumstances, and in countless other ways. You cannot put a limit on God or anything he does. He is God and he knows how to communicate with every person he created. If we listen to and obey God each step of the way, like Moses did, we will have his peace and favor as we live in the center of his will.

NUMBERS 8

Passage: "Present the Levites to the Lord as a special offering from the people of Israel, thus dedicating them to the Lord's service."

Reflection:

Like the lights in the lamp stand, Jesus shines his light forward for us to see. God's Word is a lamp to guide us and light our paths.

The Levites were a special offering to God. They were set apart, belonged to God, were reserved for God, and were claimed by God. They were purified from sin and their clothes were washed, making them right with the Lord. This is like what Jesus did for us when he died on the cross. The Levites retired at age fifty, but they could continue to serve at the Tabernacle in supportive roles. We too should continue to serve God, whatever our ages, until he takes us home.

NUMBERS 9

Passage: "But day or night when the cloud lifted, the people broke camp and moved on. Whether the cloud stayed above the Tabernacle for two days, a month, or a year, the people of Israel stayed in camp and did not move on. But as soon as it lifted, they broke camp and moved on."

Reflection:

Moses depended on God's guidance for everything. When he didn't know the answer to the question of an Israelite, he said, "Wait here until I have received instructions for you from the Lord." Moses went straight to God about the issue and asked for direction. We can also go straight to God in prayer about our issues. He may not tell us immediately what to do, but God hears us. We should wait for further instruction, just as Moses told the Israelite.

The Israelites also depended on God's guidance about where to camp and when to travel. This required them to keep their eyes on the cloud of God, watching for his sign that it was time to go. It required them to be submissive to God's will, day or night. The cloud above the Tabernacle was located at the center of the camp and

God was at the center of their lives. This is an example of how we should live the Christian life: submissive and obedient to God, and focused on him at the center of our lives.

NUMBERS 10

Passage: "This was the order in which the Israelites marched, division by division."

Reflection:

Just as God had an order to how the Israelites were to travel, he has an order to everything he does. If you are a child of God, he will hover over you and move ahead of you to show you the way. He will lead you beside peaceful streams and guide you along right paths. He goes before you and follows you, placing his hand of blessing on your head. The Lord directs the steps of the godly. He delights in every detail of their lives. Put your hope and trust in the Lord and travel steadily along his path.

NUMBERS 11

Passage: "Soon the people began to complain about their hardship, and the Lord heard everything they said."

Reflection:

The attitude of the Israelites wasn't always pleasing to God or Moses. Their complaining, screaming, and whining caused God's anger to blaze against them and caused Moses to want to give up.

Sometimes we become overwhelmed by our circumstances too and want to give up, especially when we try to do everything in our own strength. Nevertheless, God will help us and lighten our burdens if we depend on him. When the attitude of the people around you becomes toxic, change your focus to God. Let God deal with them while you rest in his peace.

NUMBERS 12

Passage: "Now Moses was very humble—more humble than any other person on earth."

Reflection:

God loves his humble servants and will defend them. When Moses's sister Miriam and brother Aaron criticized Moses, God told them all to go to the Tabernacle. There they were reprimanded by God for speaking badly about their brother, the one God trusted. Miriam was struck with leprosy and was grounded for seven days, having to live outside the camp while she learned her lesson and was humbled.

We should always be mindful of what we say. Rather than talking about people, we should talk to them. Speaking unkind words does not demonstrate love for others and it does not please God.

NUMBERS 13

Passage: "Next to them we felt like grasshoppers."

Reflection:

Focusing on the size and strength of the people in Canaan, the ten Israelite scouts only saw barriers to entering the land that God was giving them. However, Caleb, having faith in God, said, "Let's go at once to take the land. We can certainly conquer it."

Most people will see the obstacles in life as negatives, but God's children should have faith and remember that nothing is impossible for him. When we keep our eyes on God—not on what we see, other people, or our feelings—our problems will look like grasshoppers instead of giants.

NUMBERS 14

Passage: "Don't be afraid of the people of the land. They are only helpless prey to us! They have no protection, but the Lord is with us!"

Reflection:

People who defiantly abandon God, even after hearing the gospel, knowing about the miracles he performed, and seeing evidence of God's divine nature in all of creation, will not enter the Promised Land of Heaven. Because they have abandoned the Lord, he will abandon them.

However, people with a different attitude than most, who listen to God, believe in Jesus Christ, and accept him as their Savior will be pardoned of their sins. They will possess their full share of the Promised Land of Heaven by being loyal followers of Jesus. God also promises believers his protection, so don't be afraid of the people of the land.

NUMBERS 15

Passage: "When you see the tassels, you will remember
and obey all the commands of the Lord instead
of following your own desires and defiling
yourselves, as you are prone to do."

Reflection:

The Israelites wore tassels to help them remember to
obey the commands of the Lord. God knows that we are
all prone to follow our own desires, which sometimes
are sinful. However, thanks to the grace of God, our
sins, whether intentional or unintentional, are forgiven
through the sacrifice of Jesus Christ. He is God's
permanent sin offering for all people who accept him.

NUMBERS 16

Passage: "The Lord will show us who belongs to him and who is holy. The Lord will allow only those whom he selects to enter his own presence."

Reflection:

Korah, Dathan, and Abiram conspired together and incited a rebellion against Moses and Aaron. Their jealousy over God's choice to set Moses and Aaron apart as holy cost them their lives along with the lives of 250 of their followers. However, the people didn't learn anything because the very next morning they muttered against Moses and Aaron and gathered to protest. God instantly sent a plague and destroyed 14,700 people before Aaron was able to intervene.

God will defend and bless his faithful followers, and he will act against people who try to harm them. Not everyone belongs to God. Not everyone is selected to enter into his presence. Not everyone is chosen to be holy. Only people who have accepted God's son, Jesus Christ, as their Savior and Lord are called out of darkness to become royal priests—God's very own holy possessions.

NUMBERS 17

Passage: "Buds will sprout on the staff belonging to the man I choose. Then I will finally put an end to the people's murmuring and complaining against you."

Reflection:

God knows how to clearly communicate to his people. To stop the murmuring of the Israelites, God said that the staff belonging to the man he chose would sprout buds. However, God made his choice even clearer than that when Aaron's staff not only budded, but also blossomed and produced ripe almonds. Sometimes we need an answer that is crystal clear, and God knows how to provide it.

NUMBERS 18

Passage: "Be sure to give the Lord the best portions of the gifts given to you."

Reflection:

The Levites were given the special privilege of serving God at the Tabernacle. Instead of receiving an allotment of land, they were compensated with the tithes from the people of Israel. However, God told the Levites that they must also give a tenth of the tithes they received as a sacred offering to the Lord.

Christians should also give back to God the best portions of the gifts given to them by God. The first ten percent of your income is the Lord's sacred portion, and God will bless you for obediently giving back to him in this way.

NUMBERS 19

Passage: "All those who touch a dead human body will be ceremonially unclean for seven days."

Reflection:

Since sin causes death, touching a dead body caused defilement in God's eyes. However, God made a way for the Israelites to be purified through the ashes of a perfect red heifer sacrificed as a burnt offering along with a stick of cedar, a hyssop branch, and some scarlet yarn.

This offering foreshadowed the death of Christ. He died on a wooden cross. He was offered a drink on a hyssop branch, and he shed his scarlet blood for our purification. When we accept Jesus as our Savior, we are clean, pure, and sprinkled with his living water. We have eternal life. However, the defilement caused by sin continues for those who do not purify themselves through Jesus. They are unclean and cut off from God and eternal life.

NUMBERS 20

Passage: "But the Lord said to Moses and Aaron, 'Because you did not trust me enough to demonstrate my holiness to the people of Israel, you will not lead them into the land I am giving them!'"

Reflection:

Not trusting God and rebelling against his instructions is costly. It cost Moses and Aaron the chance of leading the Israelites into the Promised Land that God was giving them. In the same way, not trusting God's plan of salvation and rebelling against the conviction of the Holy Spirit to accept Jesus is costly. It will cost you the chance of entering Heaven, the eternal Promised Land.

NUMBERS 21

Passage: "Then the Lord told him, 'Make a replica of a poisonous snake and attach it to a pole. All who are bitten will live if they simply look at it!'"

Reflection:

When the Israelites requested that God hand the Canaanites, the Amorites, and the land of Bashan over to them, God heard their request and gave them victory in their battles. You are indestructible when you trust in God to accomplish his plan for your life.

When the Israelites sinned by speaking against the Lord, he sent poisonous snakes to bite them, and many people died. However, God told Moses to put a bronze snake on a pole, and all who were bitten would live and be healed if they looked at it. This was a picture of Jesus Christ who took on the sin of all people and was put on a cross. All who look at him in faith will be spiritually healed and live eternally. Jesus said, "And as Moses lifted up the bronze snake on a pole in the wilderness, so the Son of Man must be lifted up, so that everyone who believes in him will have eternal life."

NUMBERS 22

Passage: "But God told Balaam, 'Do not go with them. You are not to curse these people, for they have been blessed!'"

Reflection:

The wicked will always try to curse the godly, but they are powerless to do anything against the will of God. Whoever the Lord chooses to bless will be blessed.

NUMBERS 23

Passage: "God is not a man, so he does not lie. He is not human, so he does not change his mind. Has he ever spoken and failed to act? Has he ever promised and not carried it through?"

Reflection:

What comforting words these are for believers! We can trust God to do what he says, always. We can rest in the fact that God is with us, Jesus is our King, and he is as strong as a wild ox for his bride. No curse or magic has any power against us. God's blessing cannot be reversed for his beloved children.

NUMBERS 24

Passage: "Blessed is everyone who blesses you, O Israel, and cursed is everyone who curses you."

Reflection:

God loves Israel. He brought them out of Egypt, he fights for them, and he will devour all the nations that oppose them. The Bible was written by Jewish men inspired by the Holy Spirit. The Messiah was born to a Jewish woman and was conceived by the Holy Spirit. Jesus Christ will reign for eternity in the holy city, the new Jerusalem, which will descend out of Heaven from God. As Christians, we should pray for the safety and salvation of the people of Israel, bless Israel, and oppose those who treat them with contempt. This is the will of God.

NUMBERS 25

Passage: "The Lord issued the following command to Moses: 'Seize all the ringleaders and execute them before the Lord in broad daylight, so his fierce anger will turn away from the people of Israel.'"

Reflection:

As a result of their zeal for God, the actions of Phineas—and later Jesus—purified the people, making them right with God. Zeal is defined as fervor for a person or cause, eager desire, enthusiastic diligence, and passion. Does this describe your feelings about Jesus and following him? Are you propelled by a burning desire to please God? Do you seek to obey God and love him above all? Do you want to serve God? On the other hand, do you experience apathy, the opposite of zeal, toward God and the things of God? If so, reflect on God's blazing anger and the plague against the 24,000 people who turned away from him to worship Baal.

NUMBERS 26

Passage: "For the Lord had said to them, 'They will all die in the wilderness.' Not one of them survived except Caleb son of Jephunneh and Joshua son of Nun."

Reflection:

In Moab, God told Moses and Eleazar to record the names of all the men who were twenty years old or older and able to go to war. Not one person on this list had been among those listed in the previous registration taken by Moses and Aaron in the wilderness of Sinai.

Who made God angry for forty years? Wasn't it the people who sinned whose corpses lay in the wilderness? To whom was God speaking when he took an oath that they would never enter his rest? Wasn't it the people who disobeyed him? We see that because of their unbelief, they were not able to enter his rest. Anyone who believes in God's Son has eternal life. Anyone who doesn't obey the Son will never experience eternal life but will remain under God's angry judgment.

NUMBERS 27

Passage: "So Moses brought their case before the Lord."

Reflection:

What did Moses do when he needed direction in how to assign property for the daughters of Zelophehad? He brought their case before the Lord. That is exactly what we should do when we need help of any kind. Take it straight to the top to our Father God. He loves to help his children. Just ask.

Joshua was chosen by God to be the next leader of the Israelites after Moses. A good leader is a person who guides the people, teaches their followers, leads them in difficult times, and shepherds them. A good leader has a relationship with God, has the Holy Spirit in him or her, and goes to the Lord for direction.

NUMBERS 28

Passage: "The Lord said to Moses, 'Give these instructions to the people of Israel: The offerings you present as special gifts are a pleasing aroma to me; they are my food.'"

Reflection:

God instructed the Israelites to present offerings to him at appointed times. These offerings of animals without defects were special gifts to the Lord that pleased him. We are no longer required to sacrifice animals to God, since Jesus sacrificed his sinless life for all people. However, God still desires offerings of our time with him. Following the pattern of the Israelites, we can spend time with God each morning and evening, each Sabbath day when we go to church, and on special days like holidays. Spending time with God, putting him first, is pleasing to him and beneficial for us as we grow closer to him and more like Jesus.

NUMBERS 29

Passage: "With no defects."

Reflection:

Repeatedly, God emphasized the importance that the sacrifices which were offered to him be without defects. Jesus Christ is holy, blameless, and unstained by sin. That is why he was qualified to be the only perfect sacrifice for sinful people. His sacrifice was so complete that it only needed to be offered once. Therefore Jesus can save once and forever those who come to God through him.

NUMBERS 30

Passage: "A man who makes a vow to the Lord or makes a pledge under oath must never break it. He must do exactly what he said he would do."

Reflection:

Keeping promises is very important to God. How would we feel if God didn't keep the promises he made? These include his promises to be with us, help us, never abandon us, and never fail us. We wouldn't trust God. However, since God can be trusted to keep his Word, we can and should trust him. As children of God, we should not make promises impulsively. The promises we do make must be kept.

NUMBERS 31

Passage: "All metals that do not burn must be passed through fire in order to make them ceremonially clean."

Reflection:

Trials of life can be compared to purifying fire. God tests our faith to show that it is genuine by passing us through trials. When our faith remains strong, it brings great honor and glory to God.

NUMBERS 32

Passage: "Your sin will find you out."

Reflection:

There is no place to hide your sin from God. From the top of a mountain to the bottom of the ocean, God sees everything. God even sees the guilt hiding in your heart. The Lord says, "I am watching them closely, and I see every sin. They cannot hope to hide from me." When we stop trying to hide by confessing and turning from our sins, God will be merciful. He will forgive us and take away our guilt. Then we can say, "What joy for those whose record the Lord has cleared of guilt, whose lives are lived in complete honesty!"

NUMBERS 33

Passage: "At the Lord's direction, Moses kept a written record of their progress."

Reflection:

It is good to remember where we started in our spiritual journeys compared to where we are now. The Israelites camped at forty different places in forty years until it was finally time to cross the Jordan river into the land of Canaan. However, before they could settle in the Promised Land, they had to drive out the people, destroy their idols, and demolish their pagan shrines. Failure to do this would result in those people being "like splinters in your eyes and thorns in your sides. They will harass you in the land where you live."

As we Christians journey toward our eternal home, there will be people who harass us. God is with us at each stage of our journeys. He is leading the way and he will drive out the sinners who will have no place among the godly. Finally, God will enable us to successfully possess the Promised Land of Heaven.

NUMBERS 34

Passage: "Enlist one leader from each tribe to help them with the task."

Reflection:

When the land of Canaan was to be divided among the Israelites, God designated Eleazer the priest and Joshua as the men in charge of accomplishing this task, along with one leader from each tribe to help them.

God knows that leaders cannot do all the work alone. They need teams to help them be successful. Too often, people take on too much responsibility and try to do the work in their own strength because offers to help are few and far between. When this happens, we need to remember to "commit everything [we] do to the Lord. Trust him, and he will help [us]."

NUMBERS 35

Passage: "Murder pollutes the land. And no sacrifice except the execution of the murderer can purify the land from murder."

Reflection:

God hates murder. "You must not murder" is one of the Ten Commandments. Intentionally killing any human being, no matter their age or whether they live inside or outside of the womb, is murder.

But Jesus died on the cross to pay for all sin, including murder. Yes, even a murderer can be forgiven by God. "He is so rich in kindness and grace that he purchased our freedom with the blood of his Son and forgave our sins."

NUMBERS 36

Passage: "This is what the Lord commands concerning
the daughters of Zelophehad: Let them marry
anyone they like, as long as it is within their
own ancestral tribe."

Reflection:

God is always available to help us with our dilemmas.
We can go to him with any problem, big or small, and
he will help us know what to do. We can be confident
that God's direction is always right.

The leaders of the tribe of Manasseh came to God
with their issue concerning the land of the daughters
of Zelophehad. God validated that their claim was
legitimate and gave them the best solution, which was
accepted and obeyed. In the same way, when we seek
God's help, we need to accept and obey his answer, not
just consider it.

LAW BOOK 5

Deuteronomy

DEUTERONOMY 1

Passage: "But even after all he did, you refused to trust the Lord your God."

Reflection:

Sometimes we must take the long way home. Normally it takes only eleven days, but forty years after the Israelites left Egypt, they arrived at their destination. Why did it take so long? Because God was teaching the people to trust him.

God was angry that after he had cared for the Israelites just as a father cares for his children – leading them, guiding them, fighting for them, and loving them – they still rebelled and complained against him. The exception was Joshua, who followed the Lord completely. The quicker we learn to trust and obey God and follow him closely, the more pleased he will be, and the better things will be for us.

DEUTERONOMY 2

Passage: "Then at last the Lord said to me, 'You have been wandering around in this hill country long enough; turn to the north.'"

Reflection:

There comes a time in our lives when God comes to rescue us from our aimless wandering and gives us direction to turn to Christ. Most will reject Jesus and continue to live lives without real meaning and purpose. Only through a relationship with our Creator through his son, Jesus Christ can we do what we were created to do. Then one day we will look back on our lives and realize that the Lord has blessed us, he has watched our every step, he has been with us, and we have lacked nothing.

DEUTERONOMY 3

Passage: "Do not be afraid of the nations there, for the
Lord your God will fight for you."

Reflection:

As faithful children of God, who or what do we have
to fear? No one and nothing! Our Father is Almighty
God. Our Savior is Jesus Christ. We are indwelled by
the Holy Spirit of God. We have the entire Trinity on
our side. We can say with confidence, "The Lord is my
helper, so I will have no fear. What can mere people do
to me?"

DEUTERONOMY 4

Passage: "The Lord our God is near to us whenever we call on him."

Reflection:

Believers in Jesus Christ can have faith that whenever they call on God for anything, he is near and hears us. Our loving heavenly Father always keeps watch over us and is listening to our every thought and word.

Keeping an ongoing dialogue with God as you go through your day helps to develop an awareness of his presence. As you talk to the Lord about things and see your requests or needs met, you will know that God really did hear you and respond to your situation. What an awesome God we have, who cares about the prayers of his children! "So remember this and keep it firmly in mind: The Lord is God both in Heaven and on earth, and there is no other."

DEUTERONOMY 5

Passage: "Today we have seen that God can speak to us humans, and yet we live!"

Reflection:

The Israelites were amazed that the God of the universe spoke to them, and he has not changed. God continues to speak to us humans in a variety of ways. Because God wants to fellowship with us, he communicates in ways that we can understand. However, God expects us to fear him and obey what he says so we can continue to grow closer to him. God says, "Stay on the path that the Lord your God has commanded you to follow. Then you will live long and prosperous lives."

DEUTERONOMY 6

Passage: "Listen, O Israel! The Lord is our God, the Lord alone. And you must love the Lord your God with all your heart, all your soul, and all your strength."

Reflection:

How can we as Christians show our love for the Lord our God? Obey him. Obedience is emphasized repeatedly in the Bible. When we obey God, he can continue to bless us. When we obey God, we will be counted as righteous. When we obey God, we do what is right and good. When we obey God, all will go well with us. When we obey God, we will enjoy long lives. Show God your love by diligently obeying his Word every day.

DEUTERONOMY 7

Passage: "For you are a holy people, who belong to the Lord your God. Of all the people on earth, the Lord your God has chosen you to be his own special treasure."

Reflection:

God has chosen believers to be his children simply because he loves us. God lives among us and promises his unfailing love, blessings, and protection to those who belong to Jesus Christ. We should be thankful for this privilege and cooperate with God as he transforms our lives little by little and utterly destroys and removes anything from our lives that will lead us away from worshipping only him.

DEUTERONOMY 8

Passage: "Never say to yourself, 'I have achieved this wealth with my own strength and energy.' Remember the Lord your God. He is the one who gives you power to be successful."

Reflection:

Pride makes us think that we are responsible for our own success and wealth, but God tells us that the blessing of the Lord makes a person rich. Earthly riches are only temporary and do not bring true happiness, but the riches of a relationship with God through Jesus Christ are eternal and provide true joy, both now and forever.

DEUTERONOMY 9

Passage: "But because of God's mercy, 'I took your sin—the calf you had made—and I melted it down in the fire and grounded it into fine dust. Then I threw the dust into the stream that flows down the mountain.'"

Reflection:

Like the Israelites, we are stubborn, rebellious, corrupt, and sinful people. Repeatedly they failed to trust and obey the Lord, making him angry.

Jesus Christ took all our sins upon himself and nailed them to the cross. When we trust in Jesus and accept him as our Lord and Savior, God removes our sins as far from us as the east is from the west. Since we are still human, we may still sin in the future. However, because of God's mercy—not because we are good, for we are not—we are forgiven and unconditionally loved.

DEUTERONOMY 10

Passage: "What does the Lord your God require of you? He requires only that you fear the Lord your God and live in a way that pleases him, and love him and serve him with all your heart and soul. And you must always obey the Lord's commands—for your own good."

Reflection:

God tells his children very clearly what he wants them to do, and that it's for their own good. When you grow in your relationship with God, it's not hard to love him. Everything else flows out of your love. You want to please him. You want to serve him. You want to obey him.

God doesn't burden his children with hundreds of rules to follow. Jesus tells us the same thing: "You must love the Lord your God with all your heart, all your soul, and all your mind. This is the first and greatest commandment."

DEUTERONOMY 11

Passage: "Look, today I am giving you the choice between a blessing and a curse."

Reflection:

God gives people that same choice today. God sent his Son to the world to save the world through him. Anyone who calls upon the name of Jesus will be saved and blessed with eternal life in Heaven. Anyone who chooses not to accept Jesus will be cursed with eternal suffering in Hell. We are given the choice to make today, not yesterday or tomorrow, so be sure to make a wise one. Do you choose blessings or curses?

DEUTERONOMY 12

Passage: "And you will rejoice in all you have accomplished because the Lord your God has blessed you."

Reflection:

The things we accomplish are not of our own doing, but prideful people would say they are. Christians know that all glory belongs to God, who is able, through his mighty power at work within us, to accomplish infinitely more than we might ask or think. If you surrender your will to God, he will bless you by working out his best plan for you, your calling. Whatever it may be, it is bigger than you, it is perfect for you, and it will match your passion.

DEUTERONOMY 13

Passage: "The Lord your God will be merciful only
if you listen to his voice and keep all his
commands that I am giving you today, doing
what pleases him."

Reflection:

When others try to draw you away from the Lord
your God, do not listen. When others try to lead you
astray from God, do not listen. When others entice you
to participate in something that is not pleasing to God,
do not listen. When someone encourages you to rebel
against God and the truth of the Bible, do not listen.
The Lord is testing you to see if you truly love him
with all your heart and soul. He will be merciful to you
when you "serve only the Lord your God and fear him
alone. Obey his commands, listen to his voice, and cling
to him."

DEUTERONOMY 14

Passage: "You must set aside a tithe of your crops—
one-tenth of all the crops you harvest each
year...Doing this will teach you always to fear
the Lord your God."

Reflection:

Setting aside a tithe of your income, one-tenth of the money you earn each year, is a command of God. The ability to earn money, your job, and your income are gifts from God. Everything you have comes from him and belongs to him. Giving back ten percent is a small token of your appreciation and love. When you obey God by tithing to the local church that you attend, he will bless you.

DEUTERONOMY 15

Passage: "But suppose your servant says, 'I will not leave you,' because he loves you and your family, and he has done well with you. In that case…he will be your servant for life."

Reflection:

When you become part of God's family by the redeeming blood of Jesus Christ, you become a servant of God for life. Because of God's love for you and your love for him, it is not a burden to serve him; it's a privilege. As you honor God with your service, he will bless you in all you do.

DEUTERONOMY 16

Passage: "In honor of the Lord your God, celebrate the Passover each year in the early spring, in the month of Abib, for that was the month in which the Lord your God brought you out of Egypt by night."

Reflection:

God told the Israelites to celebrate three festivals each year to honor him. It pleases and honors God when we remember and celebrate what he has done for us. We celebrate Christmas, when God sent his Son, Jesus, from Heaven to be born on the earth. At Easter, we celebrate the resurrection of Jesus from the dead after paying for the sins of the world on the cross. By taking communion, believers remember the suffering, broken body, and blood of Jesus given for our salvation.

DEUTERONOMY 17

Passage: "This regular reading will prevent him from becoming proud and acting as if he is above his fellow citizens."

Reflection:

When the Israelites selected a king that God chose, he was to copy for himself the Scriptures on a scroll in the presence of the Levitical priests. How wonderful that we have such easy access to the Bible. We don't have to copy it word for word.

God said that the king must always keep the copy of Scripture with him and read it daily as long as he lives. Daily reading of God's Word will teach you to fear the Lord and obey him. It will prevent you from becoming proud and from turning away from God. If God said that the king must read the Scripture daily, shouldn't you?

DEUTERONOMY 18

Passage: "When you enter the land the Lord your God is giving you, be very careful not to imitate the detestable customs of the nations living there."

Reflection:

As followers of Jesus, Christians should live blameless and holy lives. You should not practice fortune telling, use sorcery, interpret omens, engage in witchcraft, cast spells, function as mediums or psychics, or call forth the spirits of the dead. These things are not of God but from Satan. They are forbidden for you and they are detestable in God's eyes. Since you have placed your faith in Jesus, trust in his love and power to take care of every detail of your life.

DEUTERONOMY 19

Passage: "If the accuser has brought false charges against his fellow Israelite, you must impose on the accuser the sentence he intended for the other person. In this way, you will purge such evil from among you. Then the rest of the people will hear about it and be afraid to do such an evil thing."

Reflection:

Sometimes being blessed of God doesn't depend on us, but often it does. God told the Israelites that he would enlarge their territory if they were careful to obey all the commands they were given: always love the Lord your God and walk in his ways. Love, obey, and walk in God's ways is a great plan to be blessed.

The law of Moses says, "life for life, eye for eye, tooth for tooth, hand for hand, foot for foot." However, Jesus said do not resist an evil person; leave revenge up to God, and do to others whatever you would like them to do to you.

DEUTERONOMY 20

Passage: "Is anyone here afraid or worried? If you are, you may go home before you frighten anyone else."

Reflection:

Fear and worry are contagious. It spreads to the people around you. When we are tempted to be fearful, we should remember these words:

> Do not be afraid as you go out to fight your enemies today! Do not lose heart or panic or tremble before them. For the Lord your God is going with you! He will fight for you against your enemies, and he will give you victory!

Remember that Jesus is with you and move from fear to fear not.

DEUTERONOMY 21

Passage: "When you are in the land the Lord your God is giving you, someone may be found murdered in a field, and you don't know who committed the murder."

Reflection:

God gives wisdom to his children for all matters. God gave instruction to the Israelites on everything from unsolved murders, to matters dealing with marriage and children, to preventing defilement of the land. So "if you need wisdom, ask your generous God, and he will give it to you. He will not rebuke you for asking."

DEUTERONOMY 22

Passage: "If you see your neighbor's ox or sheep or goat wandering away, don't ignore your responsibility. Take it back to its owner."

Reflection:

As God's children, we are to love others. Our Father says that we are not to ignore our responsibility to help our neighbors when we see them in need. God also gives examples of not mixing crops, not harnessing two different kinds of animals together, and not wearing clothes made of two different materials. In the same way, believers are not to team up with unbelievers. This is like mixing righteousness and wickedness, light and dark, Christ and the devil. That is why God told the Israelite men that they were not to marry pagan women, who would divide their faithfulness to God and cause them to sin. God wants the best for his children, and he knows that anyone who has not accepted Jesus Christ as their Savior and Lord will not obey him and will not help his children live pure and holy lives.

DEUTERONOMY 23

Passage: "But the Lord your God refused to listen to Balaam. He turned the intended curse into a blessing because the Lord your God loves you."

Reflection:

God says to "Bless those who curse you. Pray for those who hurt you. Bless those who persecute you. Don't curse them; pray that God will bless them."

The people who come into your life, even those who are difficult to be around, are placed there by God for a reason. Maybe it's to help you become stronger or more patient. Maybe it's because they need Jesus and God wants you to pray for the salvation of their souls and influence them with your life. When Balaam was hired to curse the Israelites, God "turned the intended curse into a blessing because the Lord your God loves you." God will do the same for his children today. When you stay faithful and obey God, he will turn curses into blessings because he loves you!

DEUTERONOMY 24

Passage: "Always remember that you were slaves in Egypt and that the Lord your God redeemed you from your slavery."

Reflection:

We who are God's children through Jesus Christ, should always remember that we were spiritually dead slaves to sin. Jesus redeemed us by his sacrifice on the cross, and gave us freedom and eternal life when we received his gift of salvation by faith.

DEUTERONOMY 25

Passage: "All who cheat with dishonest weights and measures are detestable to the Lord your God."

Reflection:

Cheating and dishonesty is detestable to the Lord. Jesus said, "If you are faithful in little things, you will be faithful in large ones. But if you are dishonest in little things, you won't be honest with greater responsibilities." It's not the size of the lie that matters; it's the character of the person. A liar is a liar, and that person cannot be trusted. Thankfully, we can rest in the knowledge that God is aware, and he is in control of all things.

DEUTERONOMY 26

Passage: "When the Egyptians oppressed and humiliated us by making us their slaves, we cried out to the Lord, the God of our ancestors. He heard our cries and saw our hardship, toil, and oppression. So the Lord brought us out of Egypt with a strong hand and powerful arm, with overwhelming terror, and with miraculous signs and wonders. He brought us to this place and gave us this land flowing with milk and honey!"

Reflection:

God hears our cries. God sees our hardships. God will bring his children out of Egypt into a land flowing with milk and honey. God will deliver us like he did the Israelites. Jesus said, "Keep on asking, and you will receive what you ask for. Keep on seeking, and you will find. Keep on knocking, and the door will be open to you."

Sometimes God will answer your prayers quickly, and sometimes it will take years. Nevertheless, God will always answer the prayers of his children according to his perfect will. God's Word promises, "Yes, and the Lord will deliver me from every evil attack and bring me safely into his heavenly Kingdom. All glory to God forever and ever! Amen."

DEUTERONOMY 27

Passage: "Today you have become the people of the Lord your God. So you must obey the Lord your God."

Reflection:

Just as children are to obey their parents, you are to obey your heavenly Father because you love him, it pleases him, and it's the right thing to do. It's simple: obedience brings blessings, disobedience brings discipline.

DEUTERONOMY 28

Passage: "If you fully obey the Lord your God and carefully keep all his commands that I am giving you today, the Lord your God will set you high above all the nations of the world."

Reflection:

God brings blessings for obedience and curses for disobedience. He will send them on everything in your life: work, family, finances, basic needs, safety, physical health, and mental health. Wherever you go and whatever you do will be blessed or cursed. Choose to obey the Lord and serve him with joy and enthusiasm for the abundant benefits you have received as his child. You will be blessed.

DEUTERONOMY 29

Passage: "The Lord our God has secrets known to no one. We are not accountable for them, but we and our children are accountable forever for all that he has revealed to us, so that we may obey all the terms of these instructions."

Reflection:

God made a covenant with the Israelites. He provided for them, he defeated their enemies for them, and he warned them of the curses for breaking the covenant. However, the Israelites, because of their sinful natures, disobeyed God and abandoned the covenant despite God's warnings. They turned away from God to worship and serve false gods and suffered the consequences.

We, as God's children, are accountable for everything he has revealed to us. Obey God, seek his Kingdom above all else, live righteously, and he will give you everything you need.

DEUTERONOMY 30

Passage: "Today I have given you the choice between life and death, between blessings and curses. Now I call on heaven and earth to witness the choice you make. Oh, that you would choose life, so that you and your descendants might live! You can make this choice by loving the Lord your God, obeying him, and committing yourself firmly to him. This is the key to your life."

Reflection:

We all have a life or death choice to make. If you choose to love, obey, and commit yourself to God, then you are choosing life and blessings. If you choose not to accept Jesus as your Lord and Savior, then you are choosing death and curses. The key to your life is choosing Jesus Christ. Oh, that you would choose life!

DEUTERONOMY 31

Passage: "Then my anger will blaze forth against them. I will abandon them, hiding my face from them, and they will be devoured. Terrible trouble will come down on them."

Reflection:

God knows the hearts and intentions of people. He knows that we are prone to rebel against him, abandon him, and disobey him. That is why it's important to stay close to God through praying, reading the Bible, and obeying him. When you do these things, as a true child of God through Jesus Christ, you have no reason to be afraid, be discouraged, or panic because the Lord will personally go ahead of you. He will be with you. He will not fail you or abandon you. You can be strong and courageous as you face each day and every situation.

DEUTERONOMY 32

Passage: "He is the Rock; his deeds are perfect. Everything he does is just and fair. He is a faithful God who does no wrong; how just and upright he is!"

Reflection:

God is perfect, just, fair, faithful, and upright. He surrounds, guards, carries, guides, feeds, rescues, and blesses his children. Be careful not to abandon the God who made you, because he knows how to get your attention—and it probably won't be pleasant. God wants you to listen and hear what he says. As you meditate on the truth of Scripture and apply it to your life, you will grow and be transformed into the likeness of Christ. Remember, "These instructions are not empty words; they are your life!"

DEUTERONOMY 33

Passage: "Indeed, he loves his people; all his holy ones are in his hands. They follow in his steps and accept his teaching."

Reflection:

God loves you. He holds you in his hands. He surrounds you continuously. As you follow in his steps and accept his teaching, the Lord keeps you safe and preserves you from every harm. As God's child, you are rich in favor and full of his blessings. With the eternal arms of God under you, you will be safe all your days and triumphant as the Lord drives out your enemies.

DEUTERONOMY 34

Passage: "Moses was 120 years old when he died, yet his eyesight was clear, and he was as strong as ever."

Reflection:

If we claim we have no sin, we are only fooling ourselves and are not living in the truth. Even Moses, whom the Lord knew face to face, sinned. That is why God did not allow him to enter the land promised to Abraham, Isaac, and Jacob. Instead, Moses went to the ultimate Promised Land, Heaven, to be with the Lord and his ancestors. If you hope to join Moses in the Promised Land, repent of your sins and believe in Jesus Christ, the only door to eternal life.

Printed in the United States
by Baker & Taylor Publisher Services